How To Win

The College Game

How To Win
The College Game

Proven strategies to get into college and afford it

Paul Lloyd Hemphill

To
The Winners,
My Clients

Legal Notices

This publication is not, nor is it intended to be, a source of legal or accounting advice. Information herein, in whole or in part, may be subject to varying state and/or local laws, rules and/or regulations. It is the responsibility of the user of this material to determine applicable laws, rules and/or regulations in any applicable state.

Although the information provided herein has been proven effective, neither the Author nor the Publisher assumes any responsibility for errors, omissions or contradictory interpretation of the subject matter. Nor do the Author and Publisher of this book assume any responsibility or liability whatsoever for or on the behalf of any purchaser, reader or user of the material herein. You, the said purchaser, reader or user of this material, solely assumes all responsibility for any and all such usage.

Observance of federal, state and local laws and/or regulations, and any and all other aspects of conducting business in the United States and/or any other jurisdiction, is solely the responsibility of the said purchaser, reader or user of this material.

Accounting for the many families who have been helped to receive the best possible education for their children for less money than what most people pay, we are confident that the information in this book may be used safely, legally and effectively.

Published by One White's Pond Press

Cover Design by Vaughan Davidson
Printed and bound in the United States of America
ISBN 0-9785482-0-5
First Edition: June 2006

Table of Winning Strategies

Forward

In these dramatic and changing times, paying for college is more challenging than ever.

This book meets two challenges head-on: getting into college and affording it. Most books on American colleges only deal with how to pay for it, but you get a double whammy here, a solid introduction to the financial aid AND the admissions processes. To use a baseball metaphor, the author makes a convincing argument that sound financial aid strategies will get you to first, second and third bases, but a solid admission play will get you to home plate to score and win.

Getting into college is becoming more difficult, particularly in the Northeast where you find the most expensive colleges and local students who want to remain in the region. Plus, a whole lot more students are applying to college than ever before. The powerful strategies found in this book make getting admitted easier. Pay particular attention to the section on how to apply to college. It's a real eye-opener.

The author minces no words about what you can expect before your child leaves for college, giving you a very realistic if not disturbing picture of what your money will buy. Appropriately, and with humor peppered throughout the book, the author has called the entire college admissions and financial aid processes a game that you must play by someone else's rules. It's one more reason why this book stands alone from other college how-to books.

To win the college game, this is the playbook to use.

For over 25 years I have been in the financial and college planning business. *How to Win The College Game* is one of the best books on the subject. In these changing times, this volume couldn't have come at a better time.

Jeffrey P. Morand
CollegeFundingCoach.com
Denver, Colorado

How To Win

The College Game

Introduction: A Warning

This book introduces the game colleges play at the expense of both students and parents, and reveals the least-known and perfectly legal strategies to help parents win.

Colleges are well aware that parents don't know that college admissions and financial aid constitute a game that's played by *their* rules and on *their* playing fields. Perhaps college administrators think you're either too blind to see it, too busy to notice it, or too naïve to believe it. One thing is for sure: they're too arrogant to care.

Part of their arrogance comes from many of today's college presidents and professors who are children from the counter-cultural experiment of the 1960s. They wanted to change the world with non-stop street protests, energized by an adolescent moral relativism that said, "If it feels right, do it, and don't worry about the consequences."

Today they teach that there's no such thing as evil in the world, just misunderstandings of competing ideologies. Emblematic of their close-mindedness and dogmatism, they educate as if 9/11 never happened, demand that we appreciate radicals as victims who kill people over a cartoon depiction of Mohammed, and conveniently ignore that reenlistments of American soldiers of college age are at an all-time high.

Many of these intellectual punks never grew up, and parents are unknowingly feeding their children to these frustrated lions of indoctrination and drivel, who have taken their protests from the streets and into the classrooms. Moreover, there's a lopsided majority of professors who hold the same political beliefs, marked by intolerance for opposing opinions, who use their classrooms to preach instead of teach. True to form, they hire professors who are mirror-images of themselves.

To add insult to injury, many have tenure, which is a life-time job with a guaranteed paycheck, without the attendant guarantee of intellectual integrity or academic excellence. Law professor, Alan Dershowitz, observed that "...tenured professors at major universities...are among the biggest cowards. They use tenure as a sword, but not as a shield." As they remain the Untouchables with no accountability for their words or actions, parents are required to pay their salaries.

As if to champion arrogance, the Ivy League schools act like privileged brats who bask in the heartbreak of the defeated. Instead of announcing every April the impressive profiles of the next freshmen class, they can't contain their excitement in telling the world of the high percentage of applicants they *reject*. Their hypocrisy matches their arrogance with claims of helping low-income students: in 2005 these schools managed to give full scholarships to a grand total of 46 poor students nationwide. Their shock-and-awe capacities to crush hopes and dreams and manufacture window-dressing are worn like a badge of honor.

A virus surrounds the college game. It's called commercialization. A former Harvard president believes everything in a university is for sale at the right price. Profiting from big-time college sports and research for major corporations, core academic values are being undermined, and the disease of mediocrity remains virtually untreated.

No longer do we have institutions of higher learning, but business enterprises where schools are brand names, departments are profit centers, professors are employees, parents are customers, students are consumers, and a degree is a receipt.

This book is not meant to explore this virus in depth nor does it pretend to offer antidotes. Yet it does provide a diagnosis in the form of stand-alone billboard statements from prominent critics of American higher education who are educators themselves. These insiders warn of the harm being done to the body of quality education of a generation ago.

Today the classic search for truth has been replaced by the ordinary expression of opinion, merit is mocked as students easily get A's and B's for only 10-15 hours of study per week, and lower-paid, part-time professors represent nearly half of all

American faculties. Higher education is getting lower, which makes our colleges overpriced brain dumps for our children.

Feeling overwhelmed and inadequate as individuals to do anything to improve the nation's educational values, parents and students are reduced to playing a game that hammers them financially. Like a dreadful New England winter, they are helpless to change it, so they accept and deal with it in the cold comfort it will all end soon.

The typical book on admissions and financial aid is similar to an excellent travel guide to a foreign land, but gives little indication that your destination is unfriendly territory, or that nearly every feature of your stay is dreadfully expensive. On the other hand, this book is the only one with a pre-travel advisory: it warns you of what your money is really purchasing before you leave on your journey.

The college game is already in full swing, and your financial comfort zone is headed for a huge upset. The college award letter finally arrives in late March, and you see what the school is giving your student each semester. Finally, you read the blunt reality: what you have to spend.

Nothing has the potential to wreak more havoc, or do more damage to your retirement than the college game. But the proven admission and financial aid strategies found here are perfectly legal tactics which colleges don't want you to know. After all, they're in this game to win and win big. Yet they are very comfortable on their mountain of winnings to the point of indifference to the strategies presented here, or they do little or nothing to foil your attempts to use them. Not even the popularity of this book will change their thinking. Ironically, their arrogance will allow you to use the information in these pages to score often and win big.

Paul Lloyd Hemphill
Norfolk, MA

More Words of Warning

Before You Write Those Big Checks

"Tuition is set high...and whatever else we think can be extracted from parents. In the last 10 years of committee meetings on [Boston University's] annual tuition adjustment, the only real question was, 'How much can we get away with?'"

Professor Peter Wood
"The Big Steal," National Review Online, 6/6/04

"The Chronicle of Higher Education recently released its own survey of university presidents, and its results confirm that... Five of the six most pressing issues have to do with money, and the sixth - retaining students - is only marginally related to teaching and learning."

John Merrow, "Where Are the Voices of College Presidents?"
Christian Science Monitor website, 12/21/05

"The signs of erosion on our campuses are undeniable.... it remains obsessed with a racial, ideological, and sexual spoils system called 'diversity'."

Victor Davis Hanson
Wall Street Journal, 9/27/2005

"Faculty expectations and standards have been lowered, more students come to college under-prepared, and grades have been inflated. Retention and graduation rates are considered more important than what is or is not being learned."

Richard H. Hersh
Former President, Trinity College (CT)

The End
Win Big

Your confusions, illusions and delusions about applying to college and how to pay for it are over. This book is the beginning of the end of your headaches about how to get into college and

how to afford it without taking the off-ramp to retirement delay. Watch for this pointing finger throughout the text as an alert mechanism for little known, but vital facts.

In the admissions process, this book assumes your child is competing against other students with the same grades and test scores, and with every intention of applying to the same colleges and universities. It doesn't matter what quality of school you're considering. Your student is already at a disadvantage because the competition is sameness. It's because of sameness that the top Ivy League schools reject over 85% of their applicants: they all have the *same* terrific grades and test scores. It's a damaging sameness, because it damages a student's chances of standing out from all other applicants who look the same. That makes it more difficult for the admissions office to admit your student.

What can this book do for you? It can't change your child's grades or test scores, which represent about 80 percent of the admission decision. However, what it will guarantee is that your son or daughter will receive special attention in the admissions office. I'll show you proven ways to market your child so it's easier to get into the college of his or her choice. All you have to do is follow my suggestions.

Getting into college and affording it begins with good marketing. Your student is a product, and you can use this book to market and sell your child to the colleges who are ready to buy; however, I suggest no attempt at programming your student. Neither do I proclaim a triumph of packaging techniques. Instead, I offer guidelines and suggestions on what to say and do that have proven to work. What's most important is that your student be spontaneous and personal, as well as thoughtful and focused. Plus, retirement will never again look so far away.

At this moment, you may feel like a bewildered boat passenger on rough seas, but this book will guide you in the right direction and into smooth waters. The most important advice I can give you is to allow your child to demonstrate maturity: when there are questions that need answers, have your student do the asking and get the answers. You can steer this ship, but let your student be the captain with this book as your travel guide. It'll be a beneficial life experience as he or she navigates carefully around the larger islands of Responsibility and Maturity, as well as the smaller islands of Detail, Creativity, Initiative, and Courtesy.

In the financial aid process, you will discover the boneheaded thinking of college administrators. In spite of them, the money-saving ideas and strategies here have already been tested and proven. These ideas have saved parents anywhere from $30,000 to $60,000 per child in college costs. One section of this book will demonstrate how any parent - brace yourself - can pay absolutely nothing for their child's college education, and that's without ever receiving a single scholarship from any source. There's some uncommon common sense in these pages.

On the flip side, the most harebrained suggestion I could offer is for you to do this alone. Your buying this book is like getting a driving manual for your new and expensive car. Along with this book, here's your bonus: *you get me*. Call me anytime for help in protecting your chariot of the gods.

You'll save thousands of dollars from reading this book without ever speaking to me personally. You may save even more if you call me for a free consultation.

My objective for you and your student is not simply to win, but to use the same plotting commitment that characterizes the colleges themselves: to win, and win big.

Economics 101

College Is Resume-Building Time

1. Supply and Demand. Use these next 2 pages as talking points for a serious sit-down discussion with your student about economics. Begin by stating that you may not have the money (supply) to send him/her to the college s/he wants to attend (demand). This brings you both to...

2. Basic Economic Principles: Regardless of income, one principle is a constant: your income has limits, which means you're limited to what you can spend. Before your children go off to college each fall, make certain they have a summer job that earns them spending money for the following year. By not sending them a dime during the school year will force them to learn how to budget their money, a valuable economics lesson they won't learn from a professor. This is your helpful way of immersing them in the real world that starts immediately, not after graduation. It's also a real-life, genuine selling feature that your student can put on a resume. It's a powerful statement before each job interview, "I have 4 years of experience in money-management." What's that worth to an employer?

3. Capital and Labor: Discuss the choice of a college major, and the impact a poorly chosen career can have on income, life-style - the pursuit of happiness. Discuss how an enjoyable and satisfying career can produce the money needed to purchase real freedom. This may be your biggest challenge: we live in a high-tech nation of plugged-in and cyber-connected kids who find it hard to grasp that a self-fulfilling life is not about the pursuit of things that rust. If you can define Jefferson's pursuit of happiness, that your child's life deserves meaning and value, s/he'll be more focused on things that really matter. What's that worth to both of you?

4. Competition and Production: Students grasp what it means to compete and produce. After you pick your college, fix your aim on graduating with honors. Why raise the bar of expectations? Because that's what the real world of competition does. It's also your chance to get the extra recognition for the extra effort, to earn yourself a higher degree of self-confidence and a greater sense of pride that comes with achievement. It's another powerful statement your child needs to communicate before all job interviews: "I know how to focus, how to compete, how to succeed, and I have a productive work ethic." What's all this worth to an employer? To you?

5. Forces and Indicators: Simple honesty about yourself can make a positive impression on an admissions director (not to mention all other earthlings). “In 20 years,” says a mid-West director of admissions, “the most refreshing attribute I've seen is [applicants'] recognition of their successes and failures....I'm looking for [your] ability to recognize your shortcomings and fix them.” For example, discuss a bad grade and tell the director specifically what you did, or will do, to fix it. Or, admit right up front that your SATs are poor, but you work hard and you're a good student.

To go back to the same admission officers with evidence of actual progress, begin visiting colleges not later than October of your junior year. Your goal is to stand out from all the rest, be noticed, and be admitted.

6. The Bottom Line: College is the real world. Like medical interns who train and practice their craft in real-world hospitals, college is a real practice-run for life after graduation. If they have practiced well, your children will do well, no matter what college they decide to attend.

Save $30,000
Per Child

This is so simple you'll wonder why you never read this anywhere else. Each child, if they are not physically incapacitated, can follow my easy 3-step formula:

(1) There are 15 weeks in a typical summer vacation. With a job your student can bring home each week $150. Multiply $150 X 15 weeks = $2,250 X 4 years = $9,000. That's $9,000 that stays in the parent's pocket (read: retirement).

(2) Get your student into a work-study program every year. The *minimum* money earned will likely be $1,000 a year for 10-12 hours a week. That's $1,000 X 4 years = $4,000. So far, no loans, and your child has contributed $13,000 toward their own education. That's responsibility. Incidentally, students in work-study programs typically earn better grades because they're learning time-management skills.

(3) Have your student take out Stafford Loans through the school with no payments to make until 6 months after graduation. With only the student's signature, he or she is allowed $2,650 in the first year, $3,500 in the second, and $5,500 in each of the last 2 years. It amounts to $17,150. Here's the part that causes parents to party: there's no cosigning. Here's a little perspective for contrast: $30,000 at 7% over 20 years is more than $120,000 in your retirement.

These 3 elements are what keep at least $30,000 in your retirement account *per student*, not in the college's ATM machine. Let's fantasize for a moment: you're putting 2 children through college, and my 3-step formula will keep $60,000 in your retirement account. Three children = $90,000 in savings. Not bad.

If your child commutes to a state college whose cost is $8,000 a year, this formula pays for all 4 years of college. As a parent, you pay nothing. Double not bad.

What's wrong with your student taking on some debt? Half of your life is gone already, and they have a full life to pay off the debt. Debt is good when it affords them the opportunity to establish credit. View the glass as half-full.

The average sticker-price shock of a 4-year college education today, which includes room and board, is between $40,000 for state schools and $190,000 for private schools. Warning: only 37% of college students graduate in four years, less than two-thirds finish in six. Double Warning: Approximately 50% of entering freshmen won't even graduate.

Paying for a 4-year private school in the Northeast at a cost of, say, $48,000 a year, is like paying for one BMW each year that you cannot drive, keep, trade in, or sell used. This is a novel way to frame the cost of college, but as you've learned so far you don't have to pay so much. This is a game you can win.

For starters, cut the price of a college's cost of attendance by a minimum of 20%, and you have an idea of how this financial aid game plays and what you don't have to pay. It gets cheaper as you continue reading the information in this book.

Another opportunity for savings is having your student become a resident assistant, commonly known as an RA. Available to sophomores with good grades, RAs get 3 huge benefits: (1) a single room and a meal plan worth about $8,000 a year, (2) "it's a solid job," says Katie Callow-Wright, director of undergraduate housing at the University of Chicago, which "you're able to parlay into lots of transferable skills" after college, and (3) it's demonstrable evidence of your work ethic, which will factor strongly into getting that first post-college job.

See section, ***College Work-Study***, for ways to save money if being an RA doesn't happen. When you can save at least $30,000 over 4 years, your student as an RA could save you an additional $24,000. Triple not bad. The biggest surprise of all may be found in section, ***Best Kept Secret***.

Is Your Child A WMD?

Be Careful What You Promise

A client told me that he raised a very independent-minded son. He was offered $8,500 from one college, which the son liked, and $21,000 from a school the father liked. Guess which school was chosen by independent-minded? The father told me the son's choice was going to cost him an additional $12,500 a year, or an additional $50,000 over 4 years. With money intended for the winter of his years, daddy unknowingly raised a little weapon of mass destruction of his retirement.

Because it was a family tradition, the father always promised independent-minded that he could go to the college of his choice. Tradition was getting a hernia, and his promise became an exit ramp to retirement retardation. Last we heard, the son's having a great time at school, and his grades are somewhere south of Acceptable.

TIP #1: Before your child gives you spasms of retirement heartburn, set specific parameters, such as making sure an offer for $21,000 won't be overridden by a smaller award that comes with more beer and cheer. With too much money at stake, common sense must rule the day. There are over 4,000 colleges in America, and there are a lot more colleges that'll give you and your child what you both want.

TIP #2: I hesitated with this one. This worked for a client, so she claims, who suggested that raindrops can solve a big college-selection headache. If your child wants to go to a college that has you reaching for the antacids, and your student wants to see the campus, select a rainy day to visit, and forget to bring the umbrella. Getting wet in lousy weather will insinuate a negative impression of the school. Like I said, I hesitated with this one.

“Universities share one characteristic with compulsive gamblers and exiled royalty: there is never enough money to satisfy their desires.”

Derek Bok,
Former president, Harvard University

2 Dirty Secrets

Don't Trust The People Who Send The Bill

Never assume a college president to be a master craftsman of a logical thought. One president, whose university has an endowment (cash stash) of $180,000,000, declared his school's way of increasing financial aid is to increase tuition. In other words, he's increasing your financial aid package by $500, but to do so he's increasing your tuition by $1,500. Get it? I don't either.

Note the wording in the title of this newspaper headline: "Univ of Washington Considers High Tuition-High Aid Model." There's actually a formula - a model - colleges use to raise tuitions. College presidents, once society's beacons of social conscience and enlightenment, have allowed themselves to be perceived as over-paid used-car salesmen.

Dirty Secret #1: Students who don't need as much financial aid as you do will get some of your tuition increase. Why? Either to attract smarter students or high-income students. What's wrong with this picture? Aren't smarter, low-income students supposed to get more aid? The trend, according to the National Postsecondary Student Aid Survey, indicates that many colleges are taking the ruthless approach that says, "Poor students bring in far less revenue than rich ones. To get the rich kids to pay us more money, let's entice them with some financial aid so they can pay a little less to attend, but pay a whole lot more than poor students."

Higher income families receive more financial aid at a rate four times more than students who traditionally would qualify for more aid under most need-based formulas. At the College of Greed, some traditions die with the greatest of ease.

Even though 51% of high-income families are receiving more grant aid - free money, is it possible that the standards for merit aid - higher grades and higher test scores - have loosened? Colleges will publish their high standards, but it doesn't mean they adhere to them. Perish the thought. It can easily be argued that the standards are adjusted, with moral relativism as Gatorade for the college game, in order for the money to flow more easily to school treasuries, or become one of the growing number of billion-dollar endowment universities.

Dirty Secret #2: This is the reverse of the first Dirty Secret. You could be subsidizing someone else's kid who's considered smarter than yours, but who needs *more* financial aid. The budget director at a university in Washington suggested to other colleges, "...boost tuition, but follow it with a hike in financial aid for needy students." So your child who is more talented than most gets more financial aid (read: larger discount) because you're from a low-income family on whose behalf some colleges will rob from high-income families.

Deception and cynicism permeate the rules of the college game. Colleges claim to recruit students from low-income families, but they've concluded that very few talented students come from poverty environments. A former Ivy League school admissions officer labels such a student as a "quintessential diamond in the rough." In other words, it's rare to find someone intelligent in ghettos. It seems the strategy is not to recruit more low-income students, but give the bogus impression that no child is left behind. It's far cheaper to issue a press release than award merit scholarships.

What really works for colleges is economic discrimination, no matter how ruthless it functions, or how ugly it looks. It's okay to play dirty. Appearances trump values.

There's a congressional proposal to make colleges prove they're well-run and deliver value, but that's a bad idea according to a college president and head of the Association of American Colleges and Universities. It's a proposal, he says, "that no reasonable person would want to support." So parents who work 2-3 jobs, risking their retirements everyday to pay for skyrocketing tuition increases every year, are unreasonable. Too many college presidents are simply irrational, or clueless.

"I feel deeply sympathetic," a college president declares, "with the challenge these kinds of increases pose to parents, and we do our best to keep expenses down as much as we can." Deeply sympathetic? Keep expenses down? As ABC TV's consumer reporter, John Stossel, would say, "Give me a break!" What's alarming is that this official actually believes what he says. Or does he? If he doesn't, parents are in more trouble than I thought.

A university whose endowment exceeded $776,900,000 in 2005 wrote the following statement to a student from its Office of Financial Assistance: "*Since our sources are limited* (Italics added), funds must be given to students with greater demonstrated need." After reading this twaddle, I had a John Stossel moment.

A college was shameless in a logic that was baffling and backwards. Three news stories appeared in the following sequence: the first announced its new status as a *billion*-dollar endowment university; the second said the school purchased more real estate for 214 million dollars because of its ability to pay cash up front; and the third story - brace yourself - stated that since "excellence is an expensive proposition," along with rising energy and insurance costs, tuition and fees must increase to $44,226 a year. Arrogance is a blinding mechanism that forces the illogical to appear logical.

Imagine Donald Trump demanding more money for "excellence" and expenses, when earlier he boasted of his one billion dollars in profitable investments that allowed him to pay cash up front. What colleges have earned is our skepticism.

Given the mindset of those in charge of the college game, anchored squarely in a moral sinkhole, I'm asking only one question: Are the colleges trying to fool some of the parents and students some of the time, some of the parents and students all of the time, or all of the parents and students all of the time?

You pay, you decide.

"In 18 years of in-the-trenches experience counseling kids on their college choices, I've never seen the unhappiness as widespread as it is today. If colleges don't tone down the politics, and figure out how to control ballooning costs, they run the risk of turning off enough American consumers that many campuses could marginalize themselves right out of existence."

Steven Roy Goodman,
"Hey, Profs, Come Back to Ear
Washington Post, 4 /10 /2005

Ask Tough Questions

Poke 'em In The Eye

Before reading the following, you may want to take 2 minutes to breathe into a brown paper bag.

A prestigious university in Washington DC guarantees entering freshmen the same tuition price for up to 5 years, but the price for the cost of attendance each year (including books, personal and living expenses) will be $49,320 per year. Note the cynical "feel good" advertising price-point: less than $50,000. And they'll get it all with a short, written notice instead of a short, muzzled revolver. The time has finally arrived to view the IRS as the Good Guys.

The incredibly out-of-touch financial aid director of this university announced: "Generally, families feel more comfortable knowing the financial obligations to the university in advance of matriculating." I get it. I'm supposed to feel more comfortable knowing the caliber of the gun pointed at my head in advance of your pulling the trigger.

Colleges have no incentive to lower costs since more and more students continue to apply. For the class of 2010, New York University received 35,073 applications for 4,676 slots. Increasingly, colleges exercise their own Golden Rule: your kid's going for the gold and we rule.

Ask these 3 tough questions (among many) before applying to any college:

(1) Will my child be taught by full-time professors? To cut their costs, not yours, more and more colleges are hiring part-time faculty for less pay to do most of the teaching. Nearly half of all college faculties are part-timers, up from only 22% in 1970. Plus, "universities neglect undergraduate teaching," concludes observer of American higher education, Dr. Ron Melcher of the University of Ottawa, and "excessively large classes taught by the least qualified, inexperienced, non-tenured and poorly supported faculty and delivered in impersonal ways are the new norm." Graduate students, also hired as teaching assistants, may speak English as a second language. In short, universities are outsourcing what you thought was promised in their slick catalogs.

The college catalog may well be a written warrantee that would make fiction writers blush. If a university doesn't have a set policy requiring full-time faculty members to teach your student, a small college may be a better choice. Cross your fingers.

Here's a typical college's position toward applying students: because of our huge pool of applicants, we don't need you. Your attitude must be a perfect match: I don't need your college because of the huge pool of colleges. Winning the college game requires some body armor.

(2) Do I want the best college for my child? A Princeton study concluded that bright kids do well no matter where they go to school. Regardless of the school you attend, intelligence, like cream, rises to the top. Of the newly appointed CEOs of Fortune 1,000 companies in 2005, only one CEO had an Ivy League graduate degree; approximately 10% of America's largest companies are run by Ivy League grads. Graduating from college, not where you attended, is an economic priority. Prospective students for the Ivy League are now saying, "No Thanks."

Can it be ignored that a respect for learning and character has something to do with success and the pursuit of happiness?

Because your student lives in a culture of brand names, they could obsess with going to a name-brand college. To avoid self-inflicted poverty by sending them to a college you cannot afford, indulge the obsession by purchasing the college's sweatshirt.

(3) Will I have to sell my yacht, fire two of my servants, or make another million? If your child is an academic superstar, *regardless of your income,* colleges with merit-based aid could give you a minimum of $20,000 in free money. Before applying, if you think your student has a chance, ask the college if they have merit-based aid that doesn't require a tie-in to need-based aid, and then get a satisfactory answer to Question #1. To win the college game can certainly be on your terms.

Don't sell the yacht.

"Hypocrisy, faddishness, arrogance and intellectual cowardice are among the ailments of the American university today... Amid the variety of scandals afflicting the campuses, the one constant is how the rhetoric of 'diversity' trumps almost all other considerations—and how race and gender can be manipulated by either the college president or the faculty in ways that have nothing to do with educating America's youth... There is enormous intellectual arrogance on the campus these days, manifested in condescension towards the average taxpaying citizen."

Victor Davis Hanson
Senior Fellow, Hoover Institution

The 4-Letter Word

Is A Financial Aid Office Really Helpful?

College financial aid officers (FAO) are dedicated loan activists who preach the Gospel of Loan, the sacred 4-letter word they always use before they give you any of their money. Typically oblivious to the economic demands on parents, the FAO at a prestigious college in Maine was asked about the college's reaching the $40,000-a-year mark in 2005. His clueless response: "I think there will become a point where cost is a major factor, but I don't know if $40,000 is that point." He doesn't know? Either he's buried under a mountain of cash, lost in the Maine woods, or he's not a parent.

FAOs are woefully ignorant of how to finance an education without using the 4-letter word. These are the same people who conduct financial aid nights at your local high school. Talk about the blind leading the blind. It gets worse.

The Boston Globe said that colleges are trying to "shed the image of financial aid offices and their advisers as cold and intimidating. Two years ago, [a college in Boston] renovated its financial service center to give it warmth, hoping to soothe the nerves of students and parents wrestling with how to pay for school." Translation: "As we rob you without a gun, we'll be warm and fuzzy."

They're warm and fuzzy when you lose your job and can't pay next semester's bill. Colleges may help you with additional aid (read: loan) so your child isn't forced to leave. It's nothing more than a business strategy to protect the college's keep-'em-at-any-cost retention rate. It has little or nothing to do with compassion.

When you read those great advice columns on financial aid, you'll be told that the first thing you should do is contact the financial aid office. It's great advice if you want to abuse yourself by getting into more debt with another loan.

"Colleges are having an ever-harder time making what they do comprehensible to the families footing the bills. I counsel families of all political stripes -- liberal, conservative and in-between -- and varied income levels, but they all agree on one thing: the overly politicized atmosphere on campuses is distracting colleges from providing a solid education to our young people."

Steven Roy Goodman,
"Hey, Profs, Come Back to Earth,"
Washington Post, 4 /10 /2005

The Cost Of Diversity
The Ugly Part Of Your Bill

When you read the word "diversity" in a college's advertising, grab your wallet and hold your nose. The foul odor originates from what you don't see:

Illegal Aliens Your tax and tuition dollars may pay for an illegal alien to attend class with your child. To follow 8 other states which defy federal law, your state's politicians may allow illegal aliens to pay the same in-state tuition costs at state schools as American-born state residents. Message to illegals: break our laws and we'll reward you with in-state tuition prices. With trademark credentials for pandering, many politicians act as if illegal aliens - legal-age law-breakers - add to the diversity of our colleges and universities.

Same-Sex Couples They pay less than typical parents. According to the tax laws, same-sex couples are single parents, which means a single parent can qualify for more aid. The politically-correct National Association of Student Financial Aid Administrators is *suggesting* - brace yourself - that colleges "invite same-sex couples to be honest" in filling out aid forms. When same-sex couples can simply obey the law by using one tax return to verify household income, what's their incentive to be honest in disclosing two incomes? I'm guessing the invitation to be honest will be accepted when hell freezes over.

Affirmative Action From the LA Times: "Affirmative action is highly unpopular...92% of the public (86% of blacks) agreed that admissions, hiring and promotion decisions 'should be based strictly on merit and qualifications other than race/ethnicity.' *Only bureaucrats and intellectuals...love affirmative action*" (Italics added). Your child can be the ideal candidate for a college that prides itself on its "diversity," but if the college has already met its quota of white, Asian, Jewish, Hispanic, in-state, out-of-state, or legacy students, you could be a loser. Whoever thought that a hard-working student who deserves admission for outstanding achievement could be passed over by someone else's skin color, ethnic group, or geography?

This deliberately contrived and twisted adaptation of checks and balances - send in those fat checks and we'll balance the races - was codified by the US Supreme Court when it gave the University of Michigan the green light on racial discrimination.

Colleges like to be miniature versions of the United Nations. Appearances transcend substance. A college campus *appears* to be a magnet that draws students from all over the world. What you see is not by accident, it's by design. Racial and ethnic discrimination is firmly in place in order for diversity to exist. There's little evidence that college administrators are racists, but the end results have all the ugly signs of what both cynics and the can't-we-all-get-along crowd call "good racism." In the admissions office, good racism is allowed to get in the way of proven, hard-working talent.

Apply to colleges on an Early Action basis, not Early Decision (See section, ***EarlyEarlyEarlyEarlyEarly***). And do it after Labor Day before the herd applies in December. Be the first male, female, athlete, Asian, Jew, rich, poor, out-of-state, in-state, violinist, legacy, piano player, or child-of-donor student to apply. Your chances of getting admitted are better if you're the first to begin filling a quota that matches a predetermined profile. If the quota has already been met because you were part of the herd, you're toast. Timing is everything. To score and win the college game, *apply early.*

Gender Balance With men more likely to drop out, women are assets and men are liabilities. For every 100 graduates, 58 are daughters and 42 are sons. Where T-shirts can be found to say, "Girls rule, boys drool," you'd think colleges aim for more gender balance. They don't. Kenyon College admissions dean, Jennifer D. Britz, claims that "young men are rarer, they're more valued applicants." But her college isn't running enrollment ads for more male students. Lip service trumps male recruitment efforts across the land. Colleges don't dare admit to practicing sex discrimination. In the quest for a silver lining around this cloud over men, guys can look forward to being more outnumbered by women. Cue the music of the rock 'n roll Beach Boys: "Two girls for ev-vry boy...."

Poor Students "Increasingly, discounts [scholarships] go not mainly to low-income students," claims economist Richard Vedder of Ohio State, "but to talented students prized by universities seeking to improve ratings on the athletic field or in the U.S. News & World Report rankings." Colleges prefer the rich who can pay the bills, but if they're going to give aid to a poor student, preference will go to an academic superstar. Of the nearly 60 colleges which boast of their billion-dollar endowments, only 6 have *plans* to help poor families. Or, 90% have no plans at all. See section, ***2 Dirty Secrets.***

So far, the definition of college diversity includes acceptable criminal behavior, racial discrimination, economic discrimination, and sex discrimination. To make matters worse, there's intellectual discrimination. Nearly 75% of all college professors hold the same political ideology, and evidence mounts that students who raise opposing views in the classroom risk getting lower grades. "Inbred ideological narrowness shows up," says columnist Thomas Sowell, "not only in hiring and teaching, but also in restrictive campus speech codes for students, created by the very academics who complain loudly when their own 'free speech' is challenged."

College diversity has proven to be an expensive fraud against students and parents. A radical polarization of thinking should only occur after you've been mugged on a dark street, not in a college classroom. Like it or not, to maintain a college's cosmetic diversity and its religious zeal for political correctness, instead of a constant nurturing and open exchange of ideas, it has become a student's and parent's obligation to pay through the nose.

To reduce your costs without using your nose as a conduit, you're reading the right book.

"What I have observed is a weaponizing of the university to serve the personal and political agendas of a group of administrators and their faculty allies. This is not the purpose of a university."

Professor Jon Cohen,
"Weaponizing the University: The Case of DePaul,"
American Thinker Blog, 2/1/2006

Before The Junior Year

Do Something

Begin the admissions process no later than the summer before the 9th grade. When your child's applications arrive in the room of the admissions committee 4 years later, it's Showtime: the decision to admit your student will take no longer than 20 minutes. "Today, it's a complicated and prolonged dance that begins early," says J. D. Britz, dean of admissions and financial aid of Kenyon College..."there is little margin for error: A grade of C in Algebra II/Trig? Off to the waitlist you go."

Olympic athletes begin practicing their sport 4 years before their Showtime, which takes a lot less than 20 minutes with little margin for error. Your student's preparation for admission success will take the form of fatigue, long hours, boredom, and little recognition until their Showtime. The difference is that your student will more likely win the gold, which means admission.

As an Olympic athlete must practice for only one event with total commitment, *a student should specialize in one activity or talent that demonstrates leadership and passion.* Limiting focus will allow for more time to study and to improve grades. Creating a limited but strong profile gives the colleges what they desire.

The student's mission is two-fold: to get good grades and demonstrate leadership qualities, such as initiative, organization, and commitment. While schools use grades and test scores to *qualify* you for admission, what must you do to be *accepted*? Engage in very few but quality peripheral activities, such as community service projects which you originate, organize and nurture. Don't simply show up to someone else's project; create your own.

A college admissions committee wants to see how you've managed your time and focused your efforts. Don't be a member, be an officer; don't be a player, be a captain;

if there's no debate club, start one. Colleges want to see evidence of your passion for *something*. Having a single purpose is in, being well-rounded is out.

For non-academic activities, there's a terrific website that's a cyberspace substitute for an inspiring parent. Teens relate to it and use it. It makes "community service as cool as sports." This is great news for the shy and timid student.

This website promotes young people engaging in "creating organizations, programs, and initiatives, and/or building upon existing programs." It's not so important that you join something as much as you create something that gets others to join your something. The website speaks for itself:

"**Do Something** has contracted with DeHavilland Associates [www.dehavillandassociates.com] to conduct an independent evaluation of program impact. Educators assess their students' growth on leadership, citizenship, and character skills alongside academic skill development through assessment tools provided by **Do Something**. These results are collected and analyzed by DeHavilland to document our impact.

"Educators have also told us that participating in **Do Something** leads to powerful outcomes for young people:

91% say **Do Something** increases self-confidence
61% say **Do Something** increases students' academic performance and reduces school discipline problems
87% say **Do Something** increases student and staff morale, and
77% say **Do Something** increases parental and community involvement at school."

If you don't know what to do in high school to get that all-important edge for college admission, put down this book right now and go to this website: www.dosomething.org. There's one other recommendation: revisit this site often.

If Your Child Is A High School Junior...

Don't Wait Anymore

---

1. Use These Websites Before Deciding Anything.

Go to www.myroad.com and have your student get a feel for what her/his real interests are. Take at least 30 minutes to answer 125 questions about yourself. Those interests will be matched to college majors. Then you can match those majors with the colleges that carry those majors in the geographical area of your choice. Also, go to www.princetonreview.com/college for the Counselor-O-Matic. Choosing both a college major and a matching school just got easier. Picking a school based on hearsay, an impressive website, lovely landscaping, or Thirsty Thursdays is risky. You don't want your child to be part of the 50% of entering freshmen who don't even graduate.

When you decide on your college choices, visit the campuses to get a good feeling for each school. Do you want to live in a small town or big city? Warm climate or cool? International flavor? Religious environment?

These questions can only be answered before you apply by visiting the schools which match your career inclinations. A curriculum-match has far greater importance than a brand-name school. See section, ***Ask Tough Questions***.

An overnight college visit (during the school week) always weighs in the student's favor. Plan your visit to include an appointment with the department head of your preferred major (with questions not answered on the college's website), and/or plan on attending 2 classes the next morning before you head over to the admissions office to introduce yourself. Set an appointment for a follow-up interview, if required. If you traveled a very long distance, the interview should be scheduled along with your visit. If you live not more than a 3-hour trip away, a second visit communicates a very strong interest, and that'll impress the admissions people.

The interview isn't critical any longer, but it's good face-time with the admissions person in charge of your geographical area who can put a face to your application when decision-time comes. Parents should be on the side-lines during the visit, leaving the student totally undistracted and focused on her/his concerns.

If you have a great essay (See section, ***How To Apply To College***), you'll move very fast to being accepted. Start planning your visitation dates with colleges, and apply Early Action so your last visit is no later than December of your senior year.

2. Get Better Test Scores. Hire A Private Tutor.

When a college receives applications from two students with near similar grades and comparable extra-curricular activities, guess who gets picked? It's the tie-breaker with schools that don't require SAT or ACT scores. See section, ***SAT & ACT.***

Private tutors, who can design a specific program for your student, can be more effective than a classroom with several students.

3. Take Honors & AP Classes.

You can qualify for college credit by taking these courses. If you score 4 or better on the AP (Advanced Placement) exam, you can receive college credit and save as much as $3,500 per course at a private college. Getting B's in Honors or AP classes, instead of A's in regular courses, will look better on a transcript. The colleges will see that you challenged yourself by taking something harder to get to college rather than taking something easier to get to graduation. Proof of challenging yourself beats an easy A every time. Dual enrollment would be another way to get college credit: instead of going to study hall, take a class at a nearby college.

4. Reposition Assets & Personal Finances Now.

Do you know how to lower the value of your home in the eyes of private schools in order to qualify for more aid? Do you have money saved in your child's name? Do you have money saved in a mattress? Will you put money into a universal life insurance policy?

A simple mistake in how you handle any of the above situations could be very expensive. Take control of the process, but it's a Herculean task that's better left to a professional in the field of financial aid. Only then can you use legal and ethical strategies to reduce the amount of money the schools will expect you to pay.

The last date you should reposition assets to avoid financial aid penalties is December 31st of the **junior** year when you're applying to schools that only require the FAFSA (most state colleges). The timing of repositioning avoids any look-back by a college searching for assets. Move them completely by December 31st of the **sophomore** year if you're applying to colleges which also require the CSS Profile (225 private schools). If you can't predict the colleges to which your student will apply, which is usually the case, if possible, go with the **sophomore year** deadline. See section, ***Asset Strategies***.

Notify your accountant that you want to be at the top of his list of tax returns to be completed after the first of the year. Let him know that financial aid is a very time-sensitive issue because all financial aid is awarded on a first-come, first-served basis. The same request goes to anyone else who has control over your tax return. Timing is everything.

To get a detailed by-the-month list (make a print-out) of what needs to be done during the junior year, go to this website: www.nacacnet.org. Once you're there, click on these items in the following sequence: Student Resources > College Preparation > Junior Year Calendar.

"Although we [professors] all give lip service to classroom instruction, there's simply no reward in it. Teaching doesn't advance your career. In fact, it holds you back. As Penn State University scholar James Fairweather has shown, professors who spend more time on instruction-related activities make lower salaries. The more time you devote to research, meanwhile, the more money you earn. These numbers hold constant across different types of institutions, from so-called 'Research-One' universities to liberal arts colleges."

Jonathan Zimmerman,
professor, New York University

If Your Child Is A High School Senior...

Certain Questions Must Be Asked Now

If your child hasn't started filling out college applications, do it now. There's a right way and a wrong way to do it. Most college applications will be done the wrong way. They will not meet a standard of excellence. See section, ***How To Apply To College.*** For now, ask a college financial aid office some simple questions:

What % of my need does your school meet?

Only the top colleges are likely to meet 100% of a student's financial need. Know this information in advance before your child spends time applying to a particular school that will *never* give you the money you need.

For the amount of need met by nearly all colleges, refer to www.collegeboard.com. Click in the following sequence: For Parents > College Search > College QuickFinder (and then the first letter of school's name) > Cost & Financial Aid.

Do I get the same aid package all 4 years?

A school may offer a student a great package in the first year. In the following year, it may offer the same package, but in different ratios, that is, more loans and less grants. It's not likely since such an offer smells of a bait-and-switch move. Fortunately it rarely occurs. To be on the safe side, ask the school what their policy is for the second, third and fourth years. Nail down the ratios. If the school gives you the answer you want to hear, you'll see it in the award letter. Award letters typically indicate that the school's award offer is good all four years, providing you maintain a certain grade-point average and you remain in school for four consecutive years.

Will my aid be adjusted if my need changes?

Some schools will not adjust a student's financial aid package after the first year, regardless of what happens to your finances in succeeding years. This becomes a serious problem especially if the family's income drops in the later years of college. Know the school's policy in advance so your student won't have to drop out later.

If I don't apply for financial aid before the freshman year, can I apply later?

You can always apply later. In some cases it may make sense for you not to apply for aid for the freshman year, especially if you haven't done any planning, and all of your assets are in the wrong places.

If you're a transfer student, some schools have policies of giving priority consideration to students who are already attending and receiving financial aid. If this is the school's policy, you may be shut out from getting help. Forget policy. Go ahead and appeal your award anyway. You won't know the results unless you ask.

Never volunteer any financial information on the phone to a college financial aid officer. Let your required forms do the talking. For why you shouldn't answer the phone, see section, ***After The Award Letters***.

After entering college, you'll have to fill out the FAFSA form each year. Your punishment is mandatory.

Any cut-off dates for guaranteeing financial aid?

I always recommend meeting the school's cut-off date even though the date is a soft deadline. If 1,000 applications show up on the cut-off date, do you suppose each of those applications will be reviewed that day? Hardly. But aim for the cut-off date. If you're going to be late, it looks a whole lot better if you submit a legitimate reason. The dog-ate-my-application excuse will be well received as the Laugh of the Day, but I wouldn't suggest it.

What's your policy on outside scholarships?

Most schools will substitute the grant (free) money the school was going to award you for the free money you received from, say, the local Rotary Club. So, in effect, you gain nothing by finding an outside scholarship. Who would have thought that a scholarship could be a big negative? See section, ***Scholarship Highjacking.***

Too many colleges have elevated greed to a virtue.

To get a detailed by-the-month list (make a print-out) of what needs to be done during the senior year, go to this website: www.nacacnet.org. Once you're there, click on these items in the following sequence: Student Resources > College Preparation > Senior Year Calendar.

"...there is a growing chorus of complaints from parents and students and some professors themselves---about excessively large classes, too many courses taught by grad students, and a lack of educational guidance for undergraduates."

Stanley N. Katz,
"Does college need to be reformed?"
Slate Magazine website, 11/15/2005

How & Where To Get Free Money

As Colleges Sell Sizzle, Look For Steak

With yearly tuition increases exceeding twice the rate of inflation, aid packages contain a lot more loans than grants. Before applying to Our Lady of Perpetual Increase University, consider these 6 recommendations:

1. Look for the steak, ignore the sizzle. Financial aid is nothing more than a game played by someone else's rules and on their playing field. Your opponent believes you're clueless. Protect yourself with a skeptical attitude, which comes with being better informed. Just by looking at their spectacular websites, you can conclude colleges are experts at selling sizzle in the bold expectation you won't wince at the price. Your best defense is to focus on the steak. How?

2. Ignore the frills. Colleges want to appeal, not to young, developing minds, but to their instincts. Here's the college marketing mentality: let's go for the lower common denominators to attract students. Instead of bragging of its two Shakespeare scholars, a university in New England boasts of its multi-million dollar swimming pool with a wave machine. An engineering school in New York prefers to advertise the presence of a Starbucks on campus, instead of its Nobel Laureate. The nation's # 1 party school has a new massage parlor so students can relieve stress (I'm not making this up!); and, of course, every school must have a state-of-the-art gym.

3. Go shopping... Don't waste your time traveling to a beautiful campus whose aid plan is weighted heavily towards loans. Ball State University's published aid-package ratio approximates 40% loans to 60% grants, whereas Stonehill College's is 60% grants to 40% loans. Two good schools, but one better aid package (steak). Making choices just got a whole lot easier. But where's the beef?

4. ...at this info market. Here's a huge steak tip: To discover who has better grant-to-loan ratios, go to www.collegeboard.com and do a college search. Go to the school's *Cost & Financial Aid* and look for the *average percent of need met.*

Colleges which don't disclose this statistical information are the first to tell you that they treat everyone as an individual, not as a statistic. It's the first sign that you're about to be bamboozled. That's when you know that the school should be off your radar screen of choices. Once you've made your selections, maximize your aid potential, which you will not learn from collegeboard.com.

5. Hire a private tutor. Higher SAT/ACT scores can mean more grant money from private colleges. Many will give you grants starting at $20,000 if SATs are just over 1650 and you're in the top 20% of your class. Even children of millionaires qualify for this money. Call the college's financial aid office and ask for the minimum requirements for a merit scholarship. See section, ***SAT & ACT.***

Colleges want you to believe there's more to choosing a college than just money. Don't be fooled. Colleges are in the game of marketing their own banquet of sizzle, and if Stonehill can do the same for your child as Ball State, your choice is easy. There are plenty of good schools like Ball State, but with better aid packages like Stonehill's. With growing endowments, private colleges are private banks. That's where the money is. More steak, please.

Grant and scholarship monies are awarded mostly on merit (great grades and test scores) rather than need. This money is donated by corporations, alumni, government, or the college. For the student, it's nothing more than a discount off the sticker price.

If you don't receive a discount, it may be due to (a) your child's in the bottom 50% of the entering class, (b) you don't qualify for need-based aid, (c) you qualify for lots of financial aid, but were late in submitting your aid forms, (d) you were on-time but the forms had the usual errors, omissions, and inconsistencies, or (e) you were one of the 1.8 million families who didn't fill out any forms. The life-isn't-fair response won't work. What works is doing everything right the first time. To get started, revisit item #4.

"...higher education is Teflon-coated, remarkably immune to criticism."

Gene Maeroff,
senior fellow at Teachers College,
Columbia University

Bad Advice

Unrealistic, Half True, Or Flat-Out Wrong

Beware of the so-called experts.

Advice in newspapers. From the Washington Post: "The first place experts recommend that students and their families turn is the financial aid office at their college." Not even the Washington Post knows, nor should it be expected to know, that the last people you should talk to are in the financial aid office. Why? Because these people are hard-core loan activists who work in the very expensive business of academic services and away-from-home frills. Why would you call a financial aid office when more debt will be suggested?

Here's bad advice from a Wall Street Journal article: "...it is wise to minimize the amount of funds that appear available in the eyes of financial-aid administrators by *paying off* large consumer debts, such as credit-card and car-loan balances." It's wise to minimize, but you don't have to spend. Do gifting instead. See section, ***Asset Strategies.*** Take your daddy's advice: be careful what you read in the newspaper.

Advice in books From the Princeton Review's *Paying For College Without Going Broke,* a young couple with a 3-year-old can put away $4,000 a year for 15 years and "have a college fund in excess of $55,750." But in 15 years, with costs for state colleges increasing by 10% a year, the price tag for the first year at the University of Nebraska will approximate $65,000. The Princeton Review's recommended college fund cannot even pay for the entire first year.

Advice from financial planners (aka stock brokers) From a nationally known author and financial adviser: "Since retirement accounts and your personal residence don't count against you in determining the aid for which your student will qualify, maximize your retirement contributions or make extra payments on your mortgage." This is a classic but dangerous half-truth. It's true that your residence doesn't count against you, but only with schools that require only the FAFSA. Typically, these are state schools and lesser-known private colleges. If you're applying to elite private schools, most of them will begin to salivate uncontrollably at the discovery that you have home equity. With $100,000 in equity, for example, you could lose over $5,500 in aid per year, per student, as long as the equity just sits there.

If you're making extra principle payments every month, you're walking towards a meat-grinder with private colleges. If a private school is in your future, stop making those extra payments. See section, ***Asset Strategies*** on how to reposition your home equity for more aid.

Flat-Out Wrong In a Boston newspaper article, a financial advisor told readers not to take out a larger mortgage on their home. But he doesn't state why this approach doesn't work. I have clients who have taken out a larger mortgage, and in the process of refinancing, they were able to either maintain or lower their monthly payments and withdraw enough money to pay for college. I repositioned the extra cash in a financial vehicle that's legally invisible to the schools. In many cases, this allows parents to pay less for private colleges than state schools, which is a golden nugget the financial advisor never dug up for his readers.

There aren't enough college admissions and financial aid experts in the country today. You can't even find one listed in the yellow pages. I'm not listed because most of my clients are referred to me by other clients, or they found my phone number in this book.

Your College Application

A Dangerous Test

The *Challenger* space shuttle exploded several years ago because someone didn't pay attention to a known minor detail that causes little O-ring seals to expand. Set into motion was an explosion that killed the entire crew. Here's the stark reality for all students: the admissions committee, like an employer, will give your child's application about 20 minutes for a decision, that's 20 minutes for 4 years of hard work. Any errors on the application can set into motion what will kill your student's chances for admission. Since the devil is in the details, you must dance with him precisely and gracefully.

A college application is another test to get into college. It's seductively simple, yet potentially dangerous. When an admissions officer discovers that your student didn't follow simple instructions on the application, the applicant's future is now at risk. When an application instructs you to check a box, students will circle the box, place an X inside the box, or completely fill in the box - everything but use a check-mark.

Message to students: if you can't follow simple instructions, your mistakes will distract the admissions officer from making an easy decision in your favor. Message to parents: allow your student to fill out the application, but take extreme care to scrutinize the application before submission. Your student's future could hang on this razor-thin thread.

"Never use the Common Application," says nationally-known admissions and financial aid expert, Reecy Aresty, "when the college has its own application." Otherwise, you're sending a signal to the college that their application isn't worth using. Bad signal. It's like accepting an invitation to a friend's well-prepared dinner, but you show up with your own food. Bad manners. Download the school's application using Adobe Acobat software, complete it, print it out, and have it reviewed thoroughly. Then there are schools - there's no way around it - which insist that you use only the Common Application and/or apply online.

The college application may be more important than a job application. Why? Because it decides the dock from which your student will launch his or her life's ship. That dock has to be a solid preparation platform for a future that can be met with confidence. As we say to all of our clients, "Success is in the preparation."

Your student has to look good, and one of the ways to look good is to have an application that looks like a professional document with no mistakes. It sends a potent message to the college that your student went way out of his way to pay strict attention to detail. Here's the best part: the application looks so good that it sends a subliminal and powerful signal that the student truly wants to attend their school. Colleges love to feel they're number one. Result: the applicant stands a far better chance for admission. And apply *Early Action*.

The college application is the first test-run to the first job application after graduation. You must "package" your student to the schools just as the schools package themselves to your student. The sooner it's done the greater advantage for acceptance. And your student's paperwork could set the standard by which all other applications, essays, letters of recommendations and resumes are judged. Otherwise, doing what everyone else does will have your student looking like everyone else. Admission rejection begins by running with the herd.

Treat your applying for college as if you are applying for a job. Here's the job title: Student. Your child's resume should begin in the 9th grade. Much to everyone's surprise, the Common Application, which is used by hundreds of colleges and universities, has the following requirement: "Briefly list or describe any scholastic distinctions or honors you have won since the ninth grade."

Now that your child is applying for the job position of Student, the only difference is that paychecks for this job are sent directly to the school. To make a real impact on your young adult, explain the costs involved. For example, if you're spending $25,000 a year for college, divide $25,000 by 140 days of school and the result is $178 a day, 7 days a week, or $1,250 a week. You're paying your child $1,250 a week to live, work, and play away from home. Moreover, remind your student that the weekly salary will increase by 8% each year, which is the tuition increase you'll get from the college. In addition, let your offspring know that when they party every weekend, don't have perfect class attendance, or schedule classes for only 3 days a week, remind them that it's still costing you $1,250 a week, which include days they're not studying.

A student needs a clear perspective on the effort and sacrifice a parent makes on his or her behalf. If your student doesn't produce - maintain good grades - you can give him the Donald Trump blessing: *YOU'RE FIRED!*

"All the financial aid in the world," concludes Aresty, "doesn't mean a thing without an admission ticket!" To learn more of how to receive help with your student's application, or anything else related to being accepted to the college of your student's choice, call me at 1-888-876-1863.

"...one can't help but wonder if the cost of a college education at many institutions isn't vastly out of line with the educational value delivered."

Jay Mathews,
Washington Post

How To Apply To College

Everybody Else Does It The Wrong Way

A leading expert on college admissions and financial aid is Reecy Aresty. His book, ***How To Pay For College Without Going Broke*** is a must-read by the time your child reaches 9th grade. I have taken a few of his ideas about admissions to dramatically illustrate how your student can have the decisive edge in the application process, and to beat competing students who have better grades.

This is information that will not be illustrated for you by the colleges, guidance counselors, the Princeton Review, or by any college financial aid night.

Below is part of a sample application that is submitted by hand. It's the ***wrong*** way because it's hand-written, or most applications completed online have the usual entry errors. Compare it to the ***right*** way, which appears on the next page.

Have you enrolled at any college or university since high school graduation? (U2) ☐ Yes (U1) ■ No

Enter your intended major. (Refer to page 18 for numerical code of each major; see pages 8–10 for requirements of certain majors.)

First-choice major: BUSINESS MANAGEMENT

Second-choice major: COMPUTER SCIENCE

Pre-Professional emphasis (see page 18): 708 (STILL DECIDING)

Last (family) name: HEMPHILL First (personal) name: MARK

Maiden/other name(s) you use:

6 Social Security number: 987-65-4321

Current mailing address Street address: 34 GETTYSBURG ST

City (for foreign addresses, please include postal code): NORFOLK

9-digit U.S. ZIP/Postal code: 02056-1778 Country name: UNITED STATES

Telephone number: 508-550-0000

10 Other telephone number: 508-555-1111

E-mail address: MARKHEMPHILL@MARST7.NET 13 Gender ☐ Male ☐ Female

Ethnic Origin In the boxes to the right, please enter as many letters as apply from the list on page 4. Please enter only one letter per b

Check the box that best describes your citizenship/residency.

(D)(US) ☐ I am a citizen of the United States.

(P) ☐ I am a permanent resident of the United States and a citizen of:

Note that the ***wrong***-way application has the boxes either filled in, circled, or has a line running through. The applicant is not following an easy directive to *check the box*, which appears in the third line from the bottom. If a student can't follow simple directions, here's what the admissions folks can decide, "This applicant can't follow directions. Next!"

When they discover the application below, there's a hush in the room, all eyes are fixed on this visual delight, and the committee is now disposed to enjoy this pleasant surprise. A student is about to be noticed for all the right reasons with this ***right***-way application:

Have you enrolled at any college or university since high school graduation? (U2) ☐ Yes (U1) ☑ No

Enter your intended major. (Refer to page 18 for numerical code of each major; see pages 8–10 for requirements of certain majors.)

First-choice major: Business Management

Second-choice major: Computer Science

Pre-Professional emphasis (see page 18): 708 (Still Deciding)

Last (family) name: Hemphill First (personal) name: Mark

Maiden/other name(s) you use: | **6** Social Security number: 987-65-4321

Current mailing address Street address: 34 Gettysburg Street

City (for foreign addresses, please include postal code): Norfolk

9-digit U.S. ZIP/Postal code: 02056-1778 Country name: United States

Telephone number: 508-555-0000 | **10** Other telephone number: 508-555-1111

E-mail address: markhemphill@marstt.net **13** Gender: ☑ Male ☐ Female

Ethnic Origin In the boxes to the right, please enter as many letters as apply from the list on page 4. Please enter only one letter per box.

Check the box that best describes your citizenship/residency.

(D)(US) ☑ I am a citizen of the United States.

(P) ☐ I am a permanent resident of the United States and a citizen of:

This is a work of art as compared to the ***wrong*** way. Note the tiny boxes with the required checkmarks. They're perfect. All the tiny signals are here to prove that the student goes the extra mile to do things right.

The bottom line: if you're an admissions director who has read thousands of ***wrong***-way applications, you're going to be very impressed with a student who does it the ***right*** way. And you're going to give ***right***-way students an "edge" over a ***wrong***-way student whose grades are somewhat better. That's only human, and the function of the application is to appeal to the most basic requirement of an admissions director: neatness (is next to Godliness). Neatness doesn't have the distractions as compared to what you see on the ***wrong***-way application.

What's the outcome of the ***right*** way? It indicates you care about doing it right the first time, a great life-lesson most high school seniors haven't learned yet; that you go to great lengths to present yourself well; that you care a lot to send the very best; and, that your work reflects attentiveness and correctness of detail, which schools appreciate and rarely see. In short, you've set a standard by which all other applications are judged. You've beat your competition to a pulp in the applications process. You have submitted a winning application in the college game.

Follow directions with extreme care. For example, the reader is looking to see if you put down the name of your **country** where the name of your **county** is required. It's a careless mistake. If you're near death in a hospital, you could be injected with the wrong drug because a nurse didn't take the time to read your chart carefully. Not paying attention to a little detail can kill. Since no college *needs* you, you can kill your chances of being accepted.

A work-of-art application makes the admissions folks curious to see what else is unique about your student.

Essay Most schools give far more weight to an essay than an interview. The reason is two-fold: (1) with the increasing volume of applications flooding colleges each year, there's little or no time for interviews; and (2) an essay is your only communication with the admissions committee. Only one person interviews you, whose impressions are not always reliable, but more than one reads your essay. Imagine 17-year-old Thomas Jefferson skipping a college interview, but submits an idea for starting a country with this title on his one-page essay: "Declaration of Independence." Would anyone have cared that young Tommy didn't show up? Apply to colleges with this burning ambition: write a great essay.

Admission folks know that as many as 70% of the applications they accept won't show up in September. When they see another Uncle-Bob-Was-My-Inspiration essay, after a well-practiced yawn, they're dubious about the student's desire to attend. Which begs the question: how do you convince the admissions committee that you want to attend their school and make them decide in your favor?

Most schools allow you to pick your topic, and the ideal one is what author Aresty suggests: "Why I *Must* Attend (name of school)," showing strong evidence you thoroughly researched the school, and why it matches what you want in a college. A Temple University official observed: "...a borderline candidate has a better chance at admission if they write a genuine essay that outlines precisely why they want and need to be admitted." By contrast, avoid controversial subjects and boyfriend/girlfriend breakups. Moreover, since I know of no jars of valium cookies in any admissions office, stay away from the 4 "D" Oprah subjects: Death, Disease, Divorce, and Disorder (eating or drug). Rather than impress, they depress. Furthermore, don't fake it: colleges are very good at spotting fibs and exaggerations in an essay. If you're required to write an essay that doesn't mirror the "Why I *Must* Attend" theme, purchase Harry Bauld's witty *On Writing the College Application Essay: The Key to Acceptance and the College of your Choice.*

The admissions officer can be confident the "Why I *Must* Attend" essay is from a student dedicated to attending their school. To give your essay the magic touch, weave your personality into it so the reader comes away with a strong sense of who you are. Make it *Easy Decision* time: make the admissions committee want you. When it comes down to another student having the same, or slightly better grades, but has a ***wrong***-way application and an off-limits essay, admission people have a long-standing affection for no-brainers. You win.

The great danger is to "cut and paste" your essay. "I can't even begin to count the essays that I've read," complained one admissions officer, "that say 'and this is why I want to attend

Carnegie Mellon University' [when the essay mentions another school's name].' Small details like that do make a difference. We don't care that you are applying elsewhere -- most students apply to more than one place -- but we do care that you couldn't take the time to change it to the correct university. Pay careful attention to the small details." Addressing your attractive date by another name risks immediate rejection.

Letters Of Recommendation If the student has average or below-average grades and test scores, recommendation letters need to be outstanding. Ask the teacher/writer to include personal anecdotes to demonstrate what you claim to be in your essay. Some colleges will place more value on these letters, suggesting that an adult can offer a better picture of the student's abilities and performance. Get 2 in-school letters and 2 outside letters. It's strategy to win.

Resume It can be on one page, and it should read like a supplement, not a rehash of what's already on the application. Structure it in consecutive years, and categorize sections into interests, organization and clubs, awards, summer activities, volunteer experience, travel, grades and test scores, special skills and miscellaneous. The resume should act as an image-enhancer. If you have any, colleges love newspaper clippings about you.

Business Card Imagine you're an admissions counselor, and a prospective student walks over to you and asks, "Could we exchange business cards?" How cool is that? You'd be embarrassing yourself as you look awkward, hastily searching your desk for your own card that you haven't given out since visiting your aging mother.

The business card should have the usual information - name, address and phone number - but at the top of the card should be something unique about the student, such as, *"Piano Player - Step Aside, Elton John!"* If your student has no special talent, then list good SAT scores, your large quantity of community service hours, or your best award. If you think of absolutely nothing to say, publish these words across the top of the card: "Respected by my Peers." One of my modest but clever students printed under his name, "Astonishingly Ordinary." Before leaving, hand out your card to everyone in the admissions office. Be remembered. Be admitted. Play the game.

After returning home, only the student should write a "Thank You" card to the admission director. Resist stating the standard, "It was great visiting you and seeing your lovely campus." Write something of substance that shows you put some thought into it: "I stopped by the science department, and had a good conversation with..." Follow this procedure after the letter of acceptance arrives.

To be an ideal applicant is more likely to happen if a relationship has been established before the admission decision. To show maturity the student, *never the parent*, should be in contact by phone to ask questions and by email to say "thanks" for the answer. Call with one good question at a time. Several contacts will demonstrate a high interest level. Colleges love to be noticed. It's playing to win.

In short, the information here guarantees your student a solid edge in being admitted. With all colleges watching, this is your American Idol moment, you want all members of the admissions committee voting for you, and only the best applicant wins the college game.

Since schools spend millions to look gorgeous to prospective students, the suggestions here will make your student look like a million bucks to the schools. The college game begins as a courtship, and both players must look very appealing to the other. Students who make the effort to look and act attractive will catch the eye of a school that pursues what it assumes to be a match.

As other students will have similar grades and similar test scores - sameness - *only your student will have a power presentation: a great-looking application, a convincing essay, evidence of courtesy, maturity, and credible proof that details and little things matter.* You win.

Safety Schools
Harder To Enter

Nearly 30% of all applicants to so-called safety schools like Lamar Univ (TX) and Bridgewater State College (MA) are denied admission, and roughly 40% at Humboldt State Univ (CA) and 48% at St. Leo Univ (FL) are also denied. These are colleges whose minimum SAT scores start in the basement 400s. Besides rejecting you for poor grades, you could have impressive grades and skills, and not fit the college's quest for more students from poor families, rich families, white families, black families, or albino Greek dwarf families from Wyoming. You don't have to apply to a "reach" school to be rejected. On the other hand, an excellent student may find the admissions process less stressful and easier to handle if my instruction is followed in section, ***The Math Of Admission.***

When 80% of applying valedictorians are rejected by Harvard, or when 91% of 21,000 applicants to Yale are rejected, they go to their 2nd or 3rd choice schools. This hinders those less-than-superior students who were also hoping to get into their first choices. In turn, these students frustrate those who were planning on going to their likely, or safety schools. The pecking order is very selective, not to mention that 30% more high school grads are headed for college than 10 years ago. Anyone who claims their kid will get into the college of their choice is walking on the thin ice of expectations.

Many students and parents must change their attitudes and perspectives. But how?

1. Challenge yourself: Taking unchallenging courses to get a bunch of A's doesn't work. Colleges look for A's, B's and C's in accelerated courses for evidence that a student can handle challenges. Kathy Murphy, Director of Admissions of Assumption College (Worcester, MA), sums it up: "We are looking for students who will succeed."

2. Prepare for college acceptance. High school is a time for nuts-and-bolts planning for your student's future. In a word, start no later than the 9th grade. Keep in touch often with several college admissions offices. To verify your interest in the college, many colleges maintain databases to track how many times you make contact. Find excuses to *call* each college often with one question, the answer to which cannot be found on the college's website, such as, "Will this professor be teaching this particular course next fall?" Follow-up visits are a plus. A student who often visited Northeastern became a fixture with the admissions office. She played the college game like a champion, and won. See section, ***Before The Junior Year.***

3. Community service This is the deciding factor for many schools. Most want evidence your child doesn't act as if "It's all about me!" Have someone verify in writing all those community service hours. My clients with 9th graders have a goal of 500 hours in community service. It's not overkill, it's quantity that signals quality, that is, a quality person who makes time for others' needs and concerns, not just their own. Create your own project; stick with it while demonstrating passion and leadership, and colleges will open their doors. Get great ideas for your project by going to www.dosomething.org. Of the 26,208 hours you'll breathe over 3 years, 500 hours is only 1.9% of all that time. Anyone can get an A, but not anyone can prove they became a better person.

4. Hire a private tutor to prepare for SATs and the ACT. The benefits far outweigh the cost, but many parents will nickel-and-dime their kids toward college, ignoring that every advantage for acceptance is needed. See section, ***SAT & ACT.***

5. Get a summer job. Never allow your student to work at a law firm. Colleges are repelled by gofers; however, they're impressed that your student developed a plan to make a small company run more efficiently. Nobody cares that the summer boss didn't adopt the plan, but that the student took the initiative to develop one. An impressed summer employer is a solid source for a great letter of recommendation.

Private Colleges For Less

This Is Not A Rumor

Let's say your student applies to 2 colleges, one private and one state. The private costs $40,000 a year, and the state is $10,000 a year. So far, it's an easy choice - the state school.

Let's say your expected family contribution (EFC) is $10,000, the amount the Dept of Education has decided you can afford to pay out of your own pocket. Because the private university is well-endowed with lots of money, many end up giving you enough financial aid to cover all expenses above $10,000. All you pay out-of-pocket to send your child to a $40,000/year school is $10,000. Not even Dow Jones himself would give you this kind of return.

Unfortunately, a state school in the Northeast, which is $16,000/yr (with room and board), does NOT have a lot of financial aid to give, and all they offer you is, say, $2,600. That leaves you short another $3,400. You end up paying $10,000 plus the $3,400 for a total of $13,400. The $40,000/yr school, which offered to cover all expenses over your $10,000 EFC, ends up being $3,400 less per year than the state school.

This scenario doesn't work as well with families whose AGI (adjusted gross income) is above $60,000.

The ideal financial aid scenario with a private college is to be an honor student from a poor family. Some cynics would suggest that the ideal situation for the college is awarding a bright student from a rich family because the student doesn't need the aid. All the college needs to give this student is a minimum merit scholarship, just enough to bait the talented rich student to attend. That means the college doesn't have to dish out as much money as they would for a terrific student who's destitute. See section, ***2 Dirty Secrets***.

"College used to be a 'sink or swim' environment, but today, either colleges are giving much-needed 'swimming lessons'—investing in student success—or they're allowing students to 'tread water'—giving decent grades for very little work. In the first case, students actually receive an education; in the second, they merely get a degree. It's all too easy for some students and faculty members to settle into a pattern of behavior that looks like an unspoken 'non-aggression treaty,' in which professors don't ask much of students and the students don't expect much from their professors (as long as they get A's and B's)."

John Merrow
President of Learning Matters, Inc
and co-editor of Declining by Degrees

Dumb Stuff

And Smart Stuff

Dumb: Private scholarship searches are productive.

Here's how you creatively punish your child so it doesn't look like punishment: require him or her to look up scholarships on the web. This long torturous exercise can prove to be futile. Private scholarships make up only 2% of the money available to help pay for your child's college education. The other 98% comes from the federal government, the state you live in, and the schools to which your child is applying. Therefore, you are much better off spending your time and energy going after the 98% instead of the 2%.

Dumb: Most parents making over $100,000 per year don't qualify for financial aid.

Bill Gates qualifies for financial aid. So do you, no matter what your income. He can get a government-sponsored parent Plus Loan from any number of banks. So can you. Unfortunately most parents give up before they even start, and assume they won't be eligible. In my former life, this mistake cost me over $50,000. If you fall into the category of living large (you make the big bucks), make sure you apply because everybody's eligible. See section, ***Work-Study*** on how any student, poor or rich, can receive thousands in financial aid without working.

Dumb: Financial aid is given only to athletes, minorities, and academic superstars.

"Need-based" financial aid is awarded based solely on financial need, which is calculated by taking a school's cost of attendance (COA) and subtracting the expected family contribution (EFC). That's the minimum amount the government says you can afford to pay, based on parent and student income, assets and several other factors. Whatever is left over after you subtract these two numbers is your "financial need," or maximum eligibility for financial aid at a particular school. This has nothing to do with a student's ethnic background, athletic ability, or grades. It's based on this formula:

COA (Cost Of Attendance)
- EFC (Expected Family Contribution)
= Your Financial Need

Dumb: Pay no attention to how your student compares to a prospective school's profile.

To increase your chances of getting the best possible financial aid package, it's imperative that you pick schools where your child places in the top 25% of the incoming freshman class with respect to their GPA and SAT/ACT scores. Although most schools give financial aid based on your calculation of "need," they will give preferential packaging (i.e., more FREE money, less loans) to students who place in the top 25% of the incoming class. They do this to attract better students to their school. That's why talented children of millionaires can get thousands of free dollars. Some schools will practically beg your kid to come to their school by giving you more FREE money if, for example, his/her SAT scores are better than the school's average. This will motivate the college to bribe your student to attend. In this game, it's perfectly legal to take a bribe when it's offered.

Dumb: All schools give the same amounts of money.

Some schools receive a lot of donations from alumni and corporations, and have more money to meet most or all of a student's financial need. Other schools, such as state universities, get little or no private funds, and rely solely on state and federal funds to help fill a student's need. In many cases, these schools leave students short and give them less money than they are eligible to receive. It can actually end up costing you more to send your child to a state school if they don't have the money to meet your need. See section, ***Private Colleges***.

Know each school's profile of giving money before you ever apply so you're not blown away when you get a small financial aid package from your child's top choice. Preparation will produce success. Go to www.collegeboard.com for what colleges report as their true average aid packages. The figures can be misleading, but they're good starting points. Just because a college states that it meets 80% of financial need doesn't mean they can't or won't give you more. They assume you don't know how the college game is played, and you'll accept any offer that comes close to the published figure. See section, ***After The Award Letter.***

"If you happen to be applying," concludes SmartMoney.com, "when the school is under siege from needy students, your chances of receiving a good package are much lower. The lesson: Apply as early as possible." See section, ***EarlyEarlyEarlyEarlyEarly***.

Dumb: There's no difference between "includable assets" and "non-includable assets" for purposes of qualifying for financial aid.

Certain assets are included in the financial aid formulas, which is the legal equivalent to the tax code. For example, cash, savings accounts, CDs, stocks, bonds, and other real estate are all "includable" and asked about on the FAFSA, the federal financial aid form. However, it does not ask about the value of four other financial vehicles. Put available assets into any of these four non-includable areas to qualify for more aid: (1) your home, (2) retirement plans, (3) annuities, or (4) cash-value life insurance policies. One of these hidden money safe-havens, a life insurance policy known as a modified endowment contract (MEC), offers a proven and creative way to finance a college education that is hardly known to most financial experts. It's not even mentioned on the most popular website on financial aid - FinAid.org. The MEC is tax-favored, guaranteed, safe, insured, offers a rate of return, and is 100% liquid from the first day with no penalty to get at your money. This out-of-the-box solution is very appealing to my clients. To discover if it applies to you, call me at 1-888-876-1863.

Dumb: It doesn't matter where your money is.

Where you keep your money could mean the difference between getting $10,000 in financial aid and getting nothing. For example, money in the child's name is penalized seven times more than money in the parent's name. Or, money in an UGMA or

529 savings plan can count against you as much as 25% to 100% in regards to the plan's value. If you don't know how to position your money legally for the purpose of getting more financial aid, you could end up losing thousands of dollars each year.

Dumb: Accountants can fill out financial aid forms.

CPAs and tax preparers are experts at tax planning and preparation, not financial aid planning. For example, a CPA might suggest you put some or all of your assets in your child's name. While this advice can help you save on taxes, it will cause you to lose on financial aid. Also, tax preparers are not trained to fill out financial aid forms. We have seen many cases where they unknowingly filled out these forms incorrectly (i.e., omitting social security numbers, placing the parent's assets in the wrong space, etc.), and these minor mistakes will bump your financial aid forms and cost you tons of cash. If this happens, you will have to re-submit these forms, and you may end up losing thousands in financial aid since it is awarded on a first-come, first-served basis. See section, ***FAFSA FIASCO.***

Dumb: Planning is no necessity.

To legally set up your assets so you can maximize your eligibility for financial aid, reposition them by Dec 31st of the student's junior year. Why? So that the tax return for the next year (examined by the colleges) has no record of the earnings on the sale of stocks, bonds, CDs, mutual funds - capital gains. Even if you're late, move the money. Certain other funds, such as 529s, UTMAs and UGMAs, could be repositioned in the senior year, but timing is everything. Before you make any moves, call me at 1-888-876-1863 and I'll suggest what to do in your specific circumstance.

The longer you wait and the closer it gets to your child's senior year, the tougher it gets to set up your financial situation without creating a "red flag" for the colleges and universities. It's also important to know your EFC (Expected Family Contribution) so you can start saving for it. Know which schools can give you the best packages before you start visiting and applying to them. If you haven't started planning, call me now on how to get started today.

Dumb. Really Dumb**: Do it yourself and save.**

It amazes me that people will readily use a doctor when they get sick, an accountant at tax time, a lawyer when they get sued, but suddenly when they are going to send their child to college and spend between $15,000 to $45,000 per year, parents want to save themselves a few bucks and do the admissions and financial processes themselves. Unless you've spent the last 5 - 10 years of your life doing it, there's no way you're going to know how to get the "edge" in admissions and the maximum amount of money from each school. Call me at 1-888-876-1863.

"The unnecessarily complex forms can be confusing... Students should be more challenged by their homework in college than their paperwork to receive student aid. If a student is able to fill out the form as it exists today, I don't think they should have to go to college – they should go straight to grad school."

Rahm Emanuel,
Illinois congressman

FAFSA FIASCO

The Mother Of All Forms

The FAFSA (Free Application for Federal Student Aid) form is what you must fill out in order to get any need or non-need financial aid (except for merit aid). It's easy to fill out. It's easy until your truthful entries produce disaster. For example, it's easy to indicate that your child has $900 in a savings account by answering question # 43, which pertains to the student:

> **"As of today, what is your...total current balance of cash, savings, and checking accounts?"**

Very mechanically and honestly you wrote, "$900." That was easy, but you took the bait. Before the ink dries you just walked into a trap that will be a signal to all colleges to get out their party hats and begin celebrating their gain.

Here's what you did: you told the colleges that they can penalize your child for $315 in financial aid for each year the money remains in the child's bank account. That's because the federal aid rules (the legal equivalent to the tax code) allow colleges to penalize student assets at 35% versus 5.6% of parent assets (private colleges will penalize you at 25%). The thinking at colleges goes like this: if the child has $900, then the child can use $315 to help pay for education. That means the college will deduct $315 from their financial aid package, a deduction you will never notice. That's the welcome gain you just gave the college. This is how colleges award financial aid to themselves.

Schools won't be calling you in a spasmodic fit of generosity to suggest that you transfer that $900 into the parent's account, before you file the FAFSA, so they can penalize it at only 5.6%, or $50. You can easily make the transfer the day before you sign the FAFSA, and it's perfectly legal if it's taken out of your child's savings account and put into your account. Look again at the key phrase of Question 43: "As of today..." Be sure it was *yesterday* you made a winning move of transferring the money. Timing is everything.

If your student owns custodial accounts, CDs, EE savings bonds, or mutual funds, the formula changes. You can't go by the "As of today..." time-frame. You have to remove these assets from the student's name before December 31st of the sophomore or junior years, depending on what schools your student wants to attend. See section, ***If Your Child Is A High School Junior...*** item #4.

If the student will file a tax return because there were interest earnings and/or capital gains, in order to be "invisible" in the financial aid formulas, the money must be repositioned.

The college game is to take your money, not to give you the college's money. If a single college ever calls you to suggest where to put that $900 so you can get more aid, hell will be at freezing temperatures.

The majority of FAFSA forms are submitted with errors and/or inconsistencies, which mean yours may get kicked back so you can experience the agony of filling out your FAFSA all over again. The Department of Education knows that

(1) your attitude's negative about filling out forms,

(2) you expect instant results in a fast-service culture, and

(3) you have no patience or time for filling out forms.

That's 3 strikes against you before you begin to fill out the FIASCO, er...FAFSA, not to mention you're required to fill out a FAFSA every year in order to receive financial aid. Your punishment is required for the process to work.

Plus, simple mistakes like omitting a single digit of a social security number, forgetting a middle initial, or neglecting to sign the form can actually bump a FAFSA back to you.

If this happens, you will have to resubmit it, which will take another 1-2 weeks before you can discover if you did it correctly the 2nd time. Why would you even allow this possibility to exist when there's so much money at stake?

Since most financial aid is awarded on a first-come, first-served basis, submit your aid forms accurately in the first week of January, or hire someone who's done it thousands of times. Otherwise, you take the chance of losing thousands of dollars in this entire gun-to-your-head process. The American Council on Education estimates that 1.8 million families don't fill out the FAFSA form.

Beginning in the school year 2007-2008, the aid assessment against student assets will be reduced from 35% to 20%. Accordingly, watch schools adjust their greed levels.

Colleges have the right to send a copy of your tax return to the IRS. If the tax return you sent to the college doesn't match the tax return you sent to the IRS, you risk paying a $20,000 fine or spending a year in jail. The only reason to be fraudulent with your FAFSA is to look stunning in stripes.

"The college game is a business. College websites illustrate the millions they spend on marketing their product, just as Mercedes, Rolex, and Calvin Klein do. A college's primary objective is to get your money, not give you theirs. They prefer to impress your student with a 'free' iPod whose cost is buried in your inflated tuition payments."

Paul Lloyd Hemphill

SAT & ACT

Private Tutor > Higher Scores > More Aid

Have your child start taking the SATs as soon as possible after the 9th grade. Get into practice. The objective is to make the tests routine so that the stress level of taking them later won't be so high and the results will likely be better. One-on-one coaching by the junior year is a humongous plus.

Higher scores are compulsory in an increasingly competitive environment. They're also a great way to get more financial aid. Three examples:

1. A family's son missed out on an additional $6,000 of free money because he was within 10 SAT points of the college's next plateau for additional aid. Had the family hired a tutor to improve the student's verbal skills, the expense would have been a no-brainer.

2. A family's daughter was tutored privately, and her SAT scores went from 2070 to 2250. She was accepted at a college whose SAT average was below 2250. Her scores raised the school's average, so the school saw this student as good window-dressing, that is, higher SAT students impress college-shopping parents. She was offered a Dean Scholarship for $6,000 per year - $24,000 in FREE money over 4 years. Hiring a private tutor was a very good investment.

3. A student already had SAT scores in the high 1600s. A private tutor's help pushed the SAT scores into the 1800s. She was able to apply to more selective colleges, and the less selective colleges offered her more grant money.

Tip #1: When asked why he robbed banks, Willie Sutton said, "because that's where the money is." A private school is where the money is. Apply to private, safety schools for potentially more aid. These schools want better test-scoring students so that they can tell parents like you what a quality school they have for your mon--, er, your little darling. These schools will bribe you with a more generous aid package.

Tip #2: Use higher SAT/ACT scores to apply to more selective schools. High test scores are no longer a distinguishing factor - they are a requirement. But just in case those rejection letters come in from first-choices, there can be lots of gold in those April award letters from schools with less stringent standards who really want your student for the purpose of improving their own image. Both student and college are marketing to each other. When it comes to getting more financial aid, and because the college game is a huge business, getting a good education begins with good marketing.

Not all schools require SAT scores. A religious-affiliated college in Massachusetts issued a self-serving press release, stating it will no longer require SAT scores for admission. When asked, "Why would a student submit standardized test scores if they don't have to?" Their answer: "A student might decide that his or her score gives a more complete picture of academic achievements and potential." Replace the word "student" with the word "college" and you have Truth in Advertising.

This school will use the SATs as the logical tie-breaker to award financial aid to highly competitive applicants. Check this added whopper: "We have been concerned," says the college in justifying the requirement, "about the inherent racial and socioeconomic bias in standardized testing ..." Cynics will be watching for this college to announce the rejection of its religious affiliation because of its church's “inherent bias against atheists in standardized tests of faith.” It's an elitist college using feel-good Oprah babble in their press release.

For students who don't test well, consider a smaller school that places more emphasis on grades than SAT/ACT scores. On how to get higher test scores, see section, ***If Your Child Is A High School Junior...***, item #2.

A Self-Inflicted Injury

Attending A Financial Aid Night

I don't wish this abuse on anyone - attend a high school's financial aid night. To be fair, it's not a total waste of time because, on the positive side, you may get a free pencil. On the negative side, you'll be whipped by the brutality of truth. You'll witness an eager speaker delivering an unforgiving blizzard of details on how to fill out forms and other mind-numbing paperwork. This person just so happens to be - ready for this? - a financial aid officer from a college. It's the friendly fox lecturing the unsuspecting chickens. She'll use the 4-letter word - loan - like a giant club, swinging it without mercy for two punishing hours. Your local high school neglected to warn you that tonight marks the date of your first nervous breakdown.

Why would a college financial aid person even hint at a single legal way to get more money from their coffers that are found in this book? Would a banker give you his bank's access code so you could easily rob it? Part of the college game is to keep you uninformed about the rules of the game and to get you to spend more of your money, not to give you theirs. And they love lecturing you on what loan-troths you can feed at in order to pay their overly inflated fees.

Here's a sample announcement from a high school's website on their financial aid night:

PARENT FORUM COLLEGE FINANCING SEMINAR An experienced financial aid professional will conduct the Seminar. Topics:

- The college financial aid application process;
- Completing the FAFSA;
- Resources for scholarships and grants;
- Determining financial aid eligibility;
- Student loans, parent loans, and payment plans;
- New resources for families

In sum, these nights are a lecture on the required paperwork and cost problems *with more debt as your solution.* In two hours, you will suffer perhaps the same mental anguish that Saddam Hussein receives in any two hours at the hands of his captors.

Never discussed at these high school aid nights are proven pro-retirement ways to pay for the bulk of college expenses. Never mentioned are the advantages of community colleges. God forbid! That would be discussing the competition, and in fairness to the speaker, we shouldn't expect a lecture on the competition. By the way, Bill Gates qualifies for financial aid, so "eligibility" - as suggested on the high school's website - is a non-issue.

Going to a high school financial aid night for help is a self-inflicted injury.

A Senior Moment

Colleges May Use It Against You

Senior Moment Defined: "I can coast to graduation."

Seniors shouldn't forget that the entire senior year is the most important to his/her family. Colleges are looking to see if the student is a slacker. It's their opportunity to decrease any financial aid awards if your student's grades are headed south.

Why would a student give a college an excuse to decrease aid, especially grant money which, by definition, is free money? Is your senior taking less challenging courses in the last semester? If so, prepare to give a bullet-proof reason. Colleges are watching with eagle eyes.

Be sure to warn your senior of the thousands of dollars that are at stake if they indulge their version of a Senior Moment, *getting caught up in entertaining distractions instead of focusing on good grades until graduation.* If your student isn't careful, lower 2nd semester grades can produce a financial aid disaster. Colleges can reduce the original aid package by thousands of dollars, or worse - withdraw your child's admission.

Here are two typical warning notices from many colleges in their award letters: "Your admission and financial aid awards are dependent on your successful performance until graduation." Or, "We require you to submit your final high school transcript by July 1st." Your student has been gently placed on notice; your senior's trap has been set.

If this warning condition is not included in the acceptance or award letter, is it possible the college is giving a pass to the student who's proven to be exceptional throughout high school? Call any admissions office and ask if they'll give a "pass" to your little Einstein in the last semester. Imagine hearing laughter as you wait for the answer. It's okay to have a Senior Moment when you're age 68, but not this kind at age 18.

"Let's see if we can follow the [professor's] logic: Students don't read what they are assigned, so it becomes important to assign them less reading. Talk about a race to the bottom."

Naomi Schaefer Riley
Wall Street Journal, 8/25/2005

Getting The Most Aid

Timing Is Everything

1. **Apply to 10 colleges.**

Apply to 3 types of schools: "safety" schools, "likely" schools, and "reach" schools. Pick 3 reach schools where your child has less than a 50% chance of acceptance. Then apply to 5 likely schools where you fit the college's profile and have between a 50%-80% chance of admission. Then apply to 3 safety schools that are most likely to accept your student. Parents with a high-achieving student should see section, ***The Math Of Admission.***

By applying to 10 schools you will greatly increase your ability to appeal and negotiate financial aid packages; you'll be able to play one school's offer against another's. Colleges find themselves faced with more *accepted* students not showing up in September because increasingly more students are applying to more than 6 or 8 colleges. Plus, with only 6 college choices needed to complete Step Six of your FASFA form, each school assumes you're applying to lots of other schools, and that you likely don't believe their school to be the one-and-only hallowed institution worth your wildly enthusiastic and on-your-knees consideration.

Repeat this technique in the following years by listing 2-3 schools in Step Six of the FAFSA, even if your child loves the college. Why? Give the college the impression that your student is transferring. It will give attrition-heartburn to the admissions office, which wants to maintain bragging rights on how many students remain at their college.

If you receive a financial aid package that's less than the year before, ask the college before the next semester to send your student's freshman or sophomore transcript to 3 other schools. It's perfectly legal strategy to scare extra aid out of colleges since they automatically scare extra money out of you each year. Rule of thumb: *always play hardball.* This is a very expensive game where the college's objective is to get as much of your money without giving you any of theirs.

2. Price your home.

Most families over-estimate the value of their homes. For purposes of financial aid, with exceptions like Harvard, Princeton, Emory and Carnegie Mellon, most private colleges count against you the equity in your home. And except for the University of Michigan at Ann Arbor and the University of North Carolina at Chapel Hill, state schools don't care. **Tip for the wives:** Don't allow hubby within 10 feet of the CSS Profile where it asks for the market value of the house. This is not the time for him to inflate his ego because you both made a very wise decision to buy a home whose value has increased by at least 20% in the past few years. This mistake will cost you Big Time. Instead, use this special formula, The Housing Index Multiplier, which can be found on the web:

http://www.finaid.org/calculators/federalhousing

This is based on your home's original purchase price and the year you bought it. When you see the final minimum calculation, add 5% and use your newly adjusted figure on the CSS Profile (required by most private colleges, but not required by state schools).

The true *market* value of your home is totally irrelevant and overly-inflated in the college game. Find out what your "multiplier" is and use this value for your home when applying to colleges that require the CSS Profile. Twenty-eight elite schools want you to believe that they count the market value of your house, up to 2.4 times your income, as an available asset regardless of your equity. It's a scare tactic to squeeze your lemons vigorously to get their brand of lemonade. For the legal way to prevent the lemon-squeeze, see section, ***Asset Strategies***. These schools can be found at www.568group.org.

3. Lower out-of-pocket costs now.

Assets in the wrong locations will damage your chances of getting all the money to which you are entitled. For example, never put or keep more than $67 (use any figure under $100 but over $50 - it just looks credible) in your student's name if you already qualify for need-based aid. Be sure both your student and siblings are asset-poor. Student assets in UGMA or UTMA accounts need to be repositioned very carefully. Repositioning gifted money that's already in a child's name requires a simple but little-known legal mechanism that's better discussed by calling me at 1-888-876-1863.

4. Submit financial aid forms on time.

The earliest date you can file the Free Application For Federal Student Aid (FAFSA) is Jan 1; however, many private schools will also ask you to fill out the CSS Profile, with dates that could be before January 1. Different schools have different deadlines for this form. Never miss a deadline.

5. Ignore guidance counselors and college financial aid officers.

Most high school guidance counselors tell parents to simply fill out the forms. End of story. Experienced guidance counselors are good at helping your student get into college based on personal relationships they've established with many college admission directors. But this kind of counselor, with increasing numbers of students and responsibilities that have nothing to do with college admissions, is becoming less available.

Whenever paperwork of any kind is sent to a college, send it by Priority Mail with Signature Confirmation, not Return Receipt. Demand from the high school guidance office that it provide you evidence of having sent your child's paperwork, particularly their transcript and teachers' letters of recommendations (you will send the applications and essays yourself by Priority Mail, and notify the College Board where to send the SAT scores). This could make you a world-class pain in the posterior of some guidance counselors, but why would you trust them with the small details that could sink your child's future? Give the guidance office several pre-addressed Priority Mail envelopes, and offer to pay the extra postage. Immediately after Labor Day of your student's senior year, have an understanding of what you expect from the high school guidance office.

College aid officers, or high school guidance counselors, may offer to help you apply for financial aid. Don't accept the offer. Going to a financial aid officer is like going to the IRS for help to reduce your taxes, and colleges will direct you to where you can get more loans. With the exception of merit scholarships, the schools have no interest in teaching you how to get free money from them. They want to win the college game.

Mostly all CPAs and financial planners are equally inept in the area of college financial aid.

EarlyEarlyEarlyEarlyEarly

Good & Bad

Early Action Every student should apply early, especially the struggling student. The earlier you get noticed, when you're not part of the huge herd of applicants who are pulling their hair out later, the more you can maximize your chances, learn your fate sooner, reduce a whole lot of stress, and remain focused on getting good grades in the senior year. For an Early Action decision, apply between mid-September and mid-October and obtain a decision in December. There's no obligation to attend any of the schools which accept you. This allows you to apply to several colleges without submitting the dreaded aid forms until January. If you follow my advice on the right way to apply to college (See section, ***How To Apply To College***), not only will your paperwork create the standard by which all other applications will be judged, but your chances for acceptance at the college of your choice will increase substantially.

Early Read The Academic Dean of Poker loves this one. There are some colleges which will offer to calculate your EFC (Expected Family Contribution), that is, look at your financial picture and tell you what you must spend and what your aid package will look like. The "dealer" wants to see your hand before you play it. Never give a college a hint of what you're holding because this could be the most expensive hand you'll ever play.

Early Admission This is for the brightest student. Apply at the beginning of the junior year, assuming that all requirements for high school are already completed. Colleges will compete to have bragging rights for a student of this quality. Full scholarships are not unusual. There's no requirement to attend the school once you're accepted.

Early Notification This one crawls out from under the slime. The college wants you to commit to their financial aid package well before their usual deadline, which is May 1. It looks like the infomercial that screams, "This offer is good only for the next 15 minutes!" Keep the process on your terms: wait and weigh all offers.

Early Decision This is a college's gun-to-your-head favorite. You'll be forced to sign a binding contract committing your student to that school once s/he's accepted. This makes you a hostage to whatever aid package they offer, on their terms and on their notification schedule. Not only do they hold the cards in this game, but you're giving them the entire deck to stack against you. "Early Decision is a mess," says David Hawsey, Vice President for Enrollment at Albion College, Michigan, "and students are the ones who suffer."

Why would you give any college the slightest game advantage over you when so much money is at stake? We can think of only two reasons: (1) you make over $250,000 a year and have too many assets to ever qualify for need-based aid, or (2) your daughter has threatened to marry the exterminator if she doesn't go the college of her dreams.

In a word, Early Decision stinks.

Pick A College

Curriculum is most important

Most families start planning weekend trips to visit one or more of the schools in which the student has an interest. This is how most students and families get to know each college campus, and determine if they would feel comfortable being a student there.

Traveling from campus to campus costs a lot of time and money. It also happens to be the wrong way to do things if you want to be in control of the college selection process. If your child is not applying to reach schools or the Ivy League, they have a good shot at getting into some school.

Your slam-dunk admission chances are with a community college: you can enroll by simply walking into the admissions office with a checkbook and a pulse. Graduates are generally well received as transfers by 4-year schools. See section, ***Best Kept Secret.***

Male applicants at most colleges do not have an advantage just because schools have a gender imbalance. For example, former all-women universities aren't running a national campaign to recruit more men. Yet those schools are quickly becoming a male's dream come true: two girls to every boy. See section, ***The Cost Of Diversity***.

Here's the right way to look for colleges. Instead of blindly picking schools based on academic or sports standards, or because your friend or relative's son loves a particular college for its landscaping and parties, look at three very important criteria:

(1) Does this college have the curriculum that ideally suits your student? If Princeton doesn't have what you're looking for, why apply there? Is it because you think a degree from a brand-name school will better your career prospects? Be careful. See section, ***Ask Tough Questions,*** question # 2.

(2) Does your student qualify to get into this college? This is where you find out if your student fits the school's typical freshman class with similar grades and SAT/ACT scores.

(3) Can this school meet your financial need by giving you more FREE money and fewer loans? Even a state school can cost you $15,000 or more per year when you include tuition, alcohol, books, alcohol, room and board, alcohol and other living expenses. A private university can easily run you over $40,000 per year.

After your first sticker-shock, you have 3 more years to go. And what if your child wants to go to grad school? Perhaps you're very generous - try crazy - with your retirement money.

Let's look at how the financial process works. Financial aid is awarded at most schools based on a calculation of a family's "financial need." Financial need is calculated by subtracting your EFC (Expected Family Contribution), which is the minimum amount you will be expected to pay at any school, from the COA (Cost of Attendance), which includes tuition, fees, books, room and board, travel, and chemically-induced activities. This minimum amount is determined by looking at the figures you wrote on your FAFSA.

If a private school costs $40,000 and the Department of Education says your expected family contribution is $10,000, your "need" at that school is $30,000.

$40,000 (Cost of Attendance)
- $10,000 (Expected Family Contribution)
= $30,000 (Financial Need)

It's the financial need that determines how much financial aid your family is eligible to receive; however, your need of $30,000 doesn't mean you will be offered $30,000. Pick schools that historically give the best financial aid packages. To this end the College Board website is helpful:

www.collegeboard.com

You'll discover that some schools can meet 100% or 60% of your financial need. However, most colleges can meet 100% of need. See section, ***After The Award Letters.***

When picking schools find out how much of the "need" they meet is free money, which you never have to pay back, and how much need they meet in "Self-Help" money, which includes work-study and loans you must pay back.

By knowing in advance which schools meet most of your need with more free money and less loans, you'll save yourself the hassle of applying to schools that will never give you enough money. And ask about "frontloading": does the school give you more grants in the first year and convert you to more loans later while giving you the same amount of aid? Don't ask if they frontload, just assume it by asking, "When do you start converting grants to loans after the freshman year?" If you don't get a fast, positive answer loaded with confidence and certainty from the director of financial aid, move on to your next choice college.

Planning should be done well before your student's senior year to avoid applying to colleges that will lead you gently and unceremoniously toward personal poverty.

If you're wondering how you can find this type of information, don't bother asking financial aid directors. They operate on a policy of "Don't Ask, Don't Tell." If you don't ask the right questions, they don't tell you what you really need to know. Few will volunteer any information, but they'll suggest you visit their college's website. To get more of the info you need, check the College Board website instead, and if your student is an academic star, see section, ***The Math Of Admission.***

"What is new, and troubling, is the raw power that money exerts in higher education....Nowhere in the university is this market mentality more on display than in the luring, caring, and feeding---and almost incidentally the educating----of undergraduates."

Professor David Kirp,
UC Berkeley

Scholarship Highjacking

Colleges Steal Them

A scholarship is free money, right? Well, yes and no. Let's look at 2 types:

1. College scholarships are awarded directly from the colleges themselves. You don't get a check. Instead you receive a discount on your bill (the bill is the so-called "award" letter, which illustrates how clever with words colleges can be).

2. Private scholarships come from a local group or national organization, and they're not tax-free. Here's the IRS law: *Any amount of the scholarship that is used for room, board, and personal expenses is taxable to the student as income.* Your student absolutely must keep accurate records on the money spent on tuition, college fees, school supplies, and books - everything that is connected directly to being educated. These expenses *are* tax-free. To use the money to swallow gallons of beer every weekend doesn't count. As far as expecting a student to keep records, your expectations for winning the lottery are more realistic.

These scholarships are considered assets by the colleges, and as a result, you are usually penalized at the full confiscatory rate of 100%. For example, if your scholarship is for $1,500, the colleges will subtract this amount of aid from your award package. It's like being taxed at 100%. Who knew that a private scholarship would become a cash-cow for the colleges? Those colleges who want you bad enough may substitute a pre-determined loan amount and use your $1,500 instead, suggesting how lucky you should feel to have $1,500 less in loans. In effect, the college, not you, was awarded the scholarship, a cash gift to the college with your name all over it.

To illustrate, here's one university's stated policy on your private scholarship:

"**How are private scholarships incorporated into financial aid awards?**... University need-based aid will not be adjusted when private scholarships are received unless total aid would exceed calculated need." Or, if your scholarship amount makes our original aid package more than what you need, we'll adjust the value of your aid package to our liking, not yours.

Part of the college game is the school's calculating its profits and losses on a daily basis. In other words, colleges have a total claim over any dollars you receive over and above what they normally charge you.

Colleges will punish your achievement by stealing your private $1,500 scholarship, that is, subtracting this amount from your total aid package so they can give it to a student who may not be a scholarship recipient. Cue the dead Mister Rogers: "Can you say, 'Robin Hood'?"

Here's the killer statement colleges will make in writing: "Please inform us of any scholarships or funds you expect to receive from outside sources." Never tell a college what you expect, only what you have. You may have won a scholarship, or been promised one, but if you don't have the check in your bank, there is no guarantee that it's coming, or that the check will clear. You are required to inform, but only when the check clears. You think I'm kidding? This is the college game you're playing, and you'd better play to win because your opponent is.

This is a perfectly legal counter-measure you can use against this contemptible redistribution of wealth by the colleges. Most of them are bold enough to tell you right up front that they're handling your scholarship in this manner. Plus, knowing that you're bragging to all your friends about the big scholarship you received from the local Rotary Club, they're counting on your ego to blind you from seeing what they're doing. They understand human nature. You won't know that your private scholarship was literally highjacked by the college. And the Rotary Club won't know that it was the college's unintended co-conspirator in this shameful but legal theft.

22 Income Strategies

Get More Aid + Save Money

Reducing your Adjusted Gross Income (AGI) is a viable strategy, and by doing so you'll max your ability to get more aid. Your income is assessed against you anywhere from 5 to 9 times more than your assets. Since colleges don't want you reading this info, tell your friends and accountant. It'll help you and others win the college game.

1. The Two-Income Family The lower wage earner can deduct up to 35% of salary up to the first $8,571 (Most private schools will allow your maximum to be $9,025). It's earned as an "employment allowance." This allows you to reduce your EFC (Expected Family Contribution), which is what the colleges expect you to pay.

2. Reduce Gross Income If possible ask your employer to separate your business expenses from your income. This too will reduce your AGI and EFC. Check with your accountant on the viability of this strategy.

3. If you own few assets, or possess millions in assets but have an AGI (adjusted gross income) under $50,000 a year, and you can file a 1040A or 1040EZ, your assets are excluded from the federal aid formulas and are not counted against you. You and the millionaire next door will qualify for lots of FREE money. You will pay slightly higher taxes, but you may gain a lot more financial aid.

4. Alternative Minimum Tax It qualifies as a deduction against income just like income taxes. It lowers your EFC.

5. Student Income The student will lose in financial aid 50 cents on every dollar earned over $2,500. Despite its anti-work ethic, if the aid formula works for you, stop working once you've earned $2,500. If you don't qualify for need-based aid (Is TRUMP your last name?), encourage your student to make as much money as possible = less money out of your pocket. Wealthy students should see section, ***College Work Study.***

6. Private College Trick If your student won't be earning any income, private schools (those requiring the CSS Profile) will automatically assume a freshman made $1,150 and upperclassmen made $1,400 during the summer. When the award letter comes each spring, one of these amounts will be hidden in your EFC number. This is the equivalent of one of those little annoying surcharges that pops up on a bill and can be dropped if you protest it, that is, write a matter-of-fact, not complaining, appeal letter.

7. Transfer Credit Card Debt and/or Auto Loans Refinancing or taking out a home equity loan to pay off the credit cards and autos will give you a double benefit: (1) deductibility of interest, and (2) lowering your EFC. Caution: Taking out a *line of credit* does nothing to reduce your EFC; it's reduced only by the amount used, not by the amount that was approved.

8. Student Loans Try to pay off as much of a loan of a student who has already graduated, or as much as you can while a student is still in college. This will lower your Adjusted Gross Income. Check with your accountant (1040, line 33).

9. EE Bonds If purchased after 1989, cash them in. These funds will not be part of your EFC if you indicate that the money is being spent on college tuition; the interest paid at redemption time will be tax-free. But if your income is above $119,750, forget it because the income from these bonds will be considered income by the colleges. Solution? Cash them before January 1 of the junior year, or roll them into Series H or HH bonds, report interest only when college is completed, and cash them in to help pay off student loan debt.

10. Stock Losses Take your losses in mutual funds, stocks, bonds or other investment losses during the college years up to a max of $3,000/yr (1040 Line 13). Plus, any net losses over $3,000 are carried over to future years. Note: Many private schools will recognize losses that exceed gains.

11. Start-up Business Starting your own business during the college years means a lot of start-up costs and sweet business deductions. That means a lower AGI = lower EFC = more financial aid possibilities.

12. Family Business The business pays, say $10,000, to a part-time or low-salaried family member or relative over 18 who doesn't live with you. The $10,000 is subtracted from your AGI which will result in a lower EFC and less taxes. Or, you're in the 25% tax bracket (you likely won't qualify for need-based aid) with a 15-year-old who loves computers. Hire him for $10,000 to do your company's computer work. Your tax savings = $2,500. The child would only have a $500 tax liability [$10,000 - $5,000 (zero tax bracket) x 10%] which is a $2,000 net tax savings. The savings over a 3-year period = $6,000; over 6 years = $12,000. Instead of paying the college with after-tax dollars, it's far better to hire the child and use the earnings to fund a college account that's in your name, not in the student's. See section, ***Start A Business Now.***

13. State + Local Tax Refunds To reduce your taxable income, see if you can get refunds postponed until after graduation so you can reduce your taxable income now. Hint: if you collected a refund of, say, $1,600 each year over a 4-year period, you may have lost as much as $3,000 in grants. Consult your tax person.

14. Tax Credits Most parents qualify for them. They are the Hope Scholarship Credit (up to $1,500) and The Lifetime Learning Credit (up to $2,000). You could lose some financial aid in these cases, but the gain will surely offset any loss. For each year your child is in college, get IRS Form 8863. See section, ***The 3 Little Pigs Of Financial Aid.***

15. Borrowing from a 401(k) or 403(b) With fairly low interest rates and repayment terms that are quite doable, this is tax-free "income." Call your plan administrator for guidance.

16. Medical Expenses Contact lenses, braces, cab to the doctor's office - all fit into those medical expenses that are considered in the federal aid formulas. Keep excellent records of out-of-pocket costs. The self-employed should wave their health insurance premiums like a red flag in front of a financial aid director – it's a legitimate factor as to how much more aid you can receive.

17. ROTH IRAs If the student is earning income, consider placing the money in a ROTH IRA. Retirement accounts don't count in your EFC, and no penalties or taxes have to be paid on qualified withdrawals after 5 years as long as you're 59 ½ years of age. Or, if your children are joyfully, aggressively, and enthusiastically uncommitted to work, pay them up to the maximum of $2,500 each so you can deduct the amount from your AGI. And make certain the $2,500 ends up in your account; if it's sitting in your child's account, the amount will be penalized @ 35% (beginning July 1, 2007, it'll be 20%), which means the child will lose $875 in aid each year the amount remains in the student's name.

18. Alimony/Divorce If your ex is behind in payments, get out the party hats, refreshments and celebrate: it could mean a lower EFC and more financial aid. Or, in a divorce settlement, the custodial parent should consider getting less income and more assets. Why? The child is likely to receive more financial aid. Side benefit = child gets to witness 2 mature adults place the focus where it belongs - on the child's needs, not on the parents' competing concerns. In short, everybody wins. This scenario is as optimistic as winning the lottery in the next hour.

19. Selling Your Home Gains above $250,000 are considered income by the colleges, and if you haven't purchased another home before you file the aid forms, you'll have to report the gain as an asset too. A double whammy. Solution? Don't sell your valuable house during the college years. Not selling the house will keep your EFC from going up. Selling your house with some cash left over could mean an increase in EFC.

20. Rollovers When colleges ask for a copy of your tax return, be sure to call attention to any pension or IRA rollover. You will list the rollover on line 15a or 16a of your 1040 tax return, but many colleges make the mistake of assuming that you actually received the funds. Notifying the colleges at this point in the process prevents the colleges from decreasing your financial aid.

21. Recently Unemployed or Disabled Colleges are likely to help you with more aid if you're out of work. They'll likely want proof, such as a termination notice or doctor's statement. You should contact them immediately. Ask the school to exercise what is known as "Professional Judgment." It'll signal that you know how to play the college game, and they'll likely respond in your favor.

22. Retirement Contributions What's already in your retirement account doesn't count against you, but the money you're contributing during the college years does. You may consider deferring any contributions to your retirement if you think you'll need the money to pay for a high EFC. Don't consider this option until after reading the next section, ***Asset Strategies.***

The graph below illustrates what parents can expect for a return on their investment. If education is an investment in America's future, we have a problem. Here's the irony of ironies: the solution exists only with those who have created it. In other words, we as a nation will expect the solution to come from the inmates who are currently running the asylum.

Percent of Graduating Students at 4-Year Colleges and Universities with "Proficient" Literacy

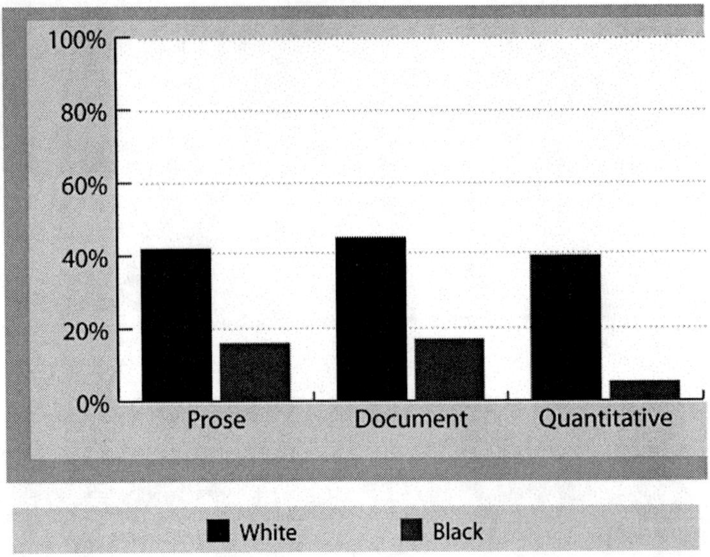

Prose: Comprehending and using information from texts such as news stories and editorials.

Document: Comprehending and using information from documents such as job applications and maps

Quantitative: Identifying and performing computations using numbers embedded in printed materials such as an interest rate schedule. *How about having the ability to interpret this graph?*

Source: J.D. Baer, A.L. Cook, S. Balch, The Literacy of America's Students, American Institutes for Research, 2006. Graph from www.educationsector.org

Asset Strategies

Reposition Your Assets To Get More Aid

Student Savings Account Hit your teenager with the first reality of college: transferring their money into your account as a loan. Why? Because most colleges reduce financial aid by 35% per year depending on how much the student has in the bank. For example, if your child has $2,000 in savings, a college will multiply $2,000 X 35% (25% at private colleges) to equal the amount of aid your student will *not* receive. If you keep an on-going balance of $2,000 in the child's account for 4 years, it gets penalized @ $700 each year. That means you'll lose $2,800 in aid over 4 years, thereby making you an unintended accessory to a robbery of $2,800 by the college.

Roth IRA If you don't want to place a child's money in your account, put it into a ROTH IRA. Only a child's earned income can be placed inside a ROTH. They can withdraw all the money tax-free after 5 years when they've reached 59 ½ years of age. All retirement plan balances are excluded from federal financial aid penalties. **Warning:** Some private colleges will consider a ROTH a student asset.

Asset Protection Allowance As a parent you can keep an amount of cash that isn't counted against you. The Dept of Education allows you money for emergencies based on the age of the older parent. For example, if you're 46 years old, $43,000 is exempt from penalty by the colleges; if you're 54, it's $53,100. If you married an old geezer, you have the benefit of a golden oldie. **Caution:** What the Dept of Ed gives, private colleges can take away. We've seen these colleges treat this "safe" money as a resource by awarding less aid. **Lesson:** When any college is asking for a copy of your tax returns, they're trolling for ways to give you less aid, not just to recheck the numbers on your forms.

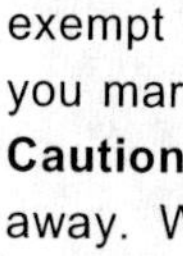

Whatever is your maximum allowance, be sure you have 50% less in evidence. Where to put the rest? See the last 2 items of this section.

529s, UGMA/UTMA Accounts & Pre-Paid Plans The slash-your-wrists negatives far outweigh the sales-pitch positives: even though these plans are assessed at 5.6% as a parent asset, you are actually penalized at a gargantuan 100%. End of story. Call any financial aid office of any private college right now to verify what I mean. But first see section, ***529s, UGMAs & UTMAs***.

Legally transfer "includable" assets into "non-includable" assets. Includable assets are penalized by the financial aid formulas. They include cash, savings, checking accounts, mutual funds, real estate, savings bonds, money-market funds, CDs, stocks, and treasury bills. Most private schools include home equity, a farm, and all the assets from the previous paragraph.

Home Equity Don't touch your home equity if you're absolutely convinced your kid's going to a state school. Such schools do not ask about your home equity, but most private schools get excited over the prospect that you have a ton of equity in your home (they don't care about your secondary residence). Home equity to a private school is a gold mine: they figure you have the gold so they can mine it to their benefit. Colleges don't care that you can cash out a lot of your equity - retirement money - to help pay for college. That means they won't have to give you a lot of financial aid. They're playing to win, and a lot of equity in your home helps them win big.

Modified Endowment Contract (MEC) What if you could take the equity out of your home so that it doesn't count against you? You can reposition it where it is guaranteed, safe, insured, and is 100% liquid at any time. One of my clients, who was paying $300 extra a month to pay down his mortgage in 15 years, decided to refinance his house for 30 years, cashed out $160,000 in equity and placed it into a MEC. As a result, his 2 children qualified for an additional $72,192 in financial aid (160,000 X 5.64% X 8 years = the penalty he removed with refinancing). And his current monthly payments remain the same. I suggest you call me before you entertain going this route. Or, consider...

Gifting If you don't want to refinance, take out the maximum amount of equity and parcel it out in the tax-free maximum amount of $12,000, as a gift to someone you trust *outside of the immediate family*. In a 2-parent home, both parents can gift a total of $24,000 to the same person. This gifting will devalue your home to a private college, which in turn will qualify you for more financial aid. Once you've settled on a school, and you've received the maximum amount of aid due to taking out the equity and exhausting the appeal process, have your trustworthy friends or relatives legally gift the money back to you. If you gifted $100,000, you'd qualify for $5,600 in financial aid *per child*. Of course, you'll pay interest on the loan you took out, but it'll be more than offset by the aid you receive.

Repeat this process each year your children are in college. This approach works very well with close-knit families where trust is a sacred bond. In the example above, 2 children in college could get you an additional $11,200 in financial aid in one year. Are you salivating yet?

The strategy of gifting doesn't have to be limited to reducing home equity. You can gift whatever money you have in bank accounts, stocks, bonds, CDs, or mutual funds. The objective is to have all the appearances of being asset poor, destitute, or broke. It's all perfectly legal in a game that's designed to beat you, but it's a game you can win.

Equity Indexed Annuities (EIA) This is a non-includable asset sold by insurance companies. It's nothing more than a savings account with a very attractive feature: whatever money you put into them is subject to the upward moves of the market, never the down ones. It's anti-gravitational. You participate only in the gains of the market, never its losses. If the market goes up and you gain 7% or 8% over a 12-month period, say, $700 on $10,000 invested, your new $10,700 stays right where it is if the market takes a dive in the following year. Once it starts to go back up and the market's made a gain for the next year, your $10,700 also goes up in value. Bottom line: you can't lose any money in a bad year, but you can earn money in a good year. Or, there's only upside potential with no downside risk. To avoid risking all of your invested money, we encourage our clients to put at least some of their portfolio assets into an EIA.

Some elite colleges (MIT and Bates come to mind) will ask Section Q questions from the CSS Profile to determine if a parent has an annuity or whole life [illegible] Before applying to any of these schools, call the [illegible] aid office to ask if they use the Section Q questionnaire.

To reduce the cost of college, there are 2 financial vehicles I recommend most for repositioned assets: MECs and EIAs. Caution: there are very few companies which can give you these vehicles with the benefits I described, and there are even fewer people who can guide you in their purchase. See section, ***If Your Aid Isn't Enough,*** last paragraph. Call me to discuss what may work better for you: 1-888-876-1863.

529s, UTMAs & UGMAs
Avoid Them

Don't buy a 529 Plan. All 529 plans reduce your financial aid. Uncle Sam doesn't tax you to use these funds, but the colleges do. "Sound complicated? It is." So says the head honcho of a 529 marketing website. "And we are only talking about the federal financial aid rules here -- each school can (and most will) set its own rules when handing out its own need-based scholarships, and many schools are starting to adjust awards when they discover 529 accounts in the family."

In other words, you won't know how each school will structure your financial aid package until after they see *your* 529. Then it's time to cross your fingers, arms, legs, and eyeballs. Is this any way to purchase a college-aid plan, filled with mystery, at the mercy of each college's own policy toward 529s, and subject to regulatory crackdowns on the marketing practices of brokers?

Assume the worst. Colleges will treat your 529 as a far-away ATM machine in your possession with the college's name all over it. Let's say your 529 has $10,000. Colleges will penalize you by making you spend the full amount, which is a bona fide penalty of 100%. That means you will lose $10,000 in financial aid because, from the perspective of the colleges, you already have $10,000 earmarked for education. That's the purpose of a 529 plan: not some, but *all* the money goes to paying for college. With the best of intentions, your 529 became a scholarship program you created all by yourself. Visualize the giddiness of everyone in the college's financial aid office upon discovery of your 529 plan.

Call any college financial aid office, ask for the expert on 529s, and ask when your 529 becomes an "asset" versus a "resource." It's actually both. Caution: Baldness is in your immediate future. While on the phone, prepare to pull your hair out as you try desperately to understand convoluted explanations. Then go for the impossible: get an email explanation on how the college will treat *your* 529 Plan. As the 529 marketing website says, it's complicated. The KISS formula (Keep It Simple Stupid)

00 of financial aid went out the window the day you ding your 529 plan.

529 is a reverse subsidy program. Instead of colleges aid, you're giving them aid. It's in the form of freeing up $10,000 for the colleges to give to someone else. In this example, the $10,000 you would have received, if you did not own a 529 plan, is parceled out to other students who don't have one. And because the 529s are tax-free at spending time, people easily buy the 529 sales pitch without ever questioning the pitcher.

A 529 in a younger sibling's name will also be counted against the entering student. More damage. Or, you thought it was clever to transfer ownership to the student's grandparent, thereby making the asset someone else's. If and when a college, which requires the CSS Profile, asks a question from its Section Q, damage again: the school can reduce your financial aid dollar for dollar. Big hurt.

Don't you just marvel at how colleges can be creative with your money? As Paul Harvey would say, "Now you know the rest of the story."

TIP: Call colleges to verify their policy on 529s (Get out the antacids and don't forget the helmet).

UGMAs and UTMAs (Uniform Gift and Uniform Transfer to Minors Act Accounts) are trust accounts that also have punishment-promise because they're considered a student asset. You're hit with an assessment of 25% at private schools or 35% at state schools. Using our $10,000 example, you stand to lose a minimum of $2,500 in financial aid in the first college year. That's a generous subsidy for another student who doesn't own an UGMA. UTMAs work the same way. Warning: this money is an irrevocable asset of the child. That means they own it, and when they reach legal age (18 or 21), they can spend it any way they want. If you spend it, you can be sued by the child later for the entire amount. Have you hugged your child today?

Pre-Paid Tuition Plans: You're slammed and rolled at a full 100%, dollar-for-dollar. In our $10,000 example, you would lose

$10,000 in financial aid because you have this prepaid tuition plan. Okay...it still beats having bought swamp land in Florida.

For information on how to legally reposition the money in these programs, to get off the college's radar screen of penalties and assessments, and qualify for more aid, see section, ***Asset Strategies***. And call me at 1-888-876-1863.

If your child has a job, consider placing the earnings into a ROTH IRA. Because ROTHs are purchased with after-tax dollars, you can withdraw money after 5 years without being taxed once you reach 59 ½ years of age. Plus, IRAs are not included in the financial aid formulas, although some prestigious colleges may ask if you own one. If you do, well, you know the rest of the story.

"I have found that a demanding professor who might be a good teacher but refuses to do the 'dog and pony show' for the students, and grades without inflation, will tend to get low evaluations [from students]. However, the professor who attempts to be personable with the students while asking little academically, and inflates grades, will get high evaluations. Sounds a little like the prisoners are running the prison, doesn't it?"

R. Terry Ervin, Chair
Department of Family and Consumer Sciences, and Agriculture
Eastern New Mexico University

Start A Business Now

More Financial Aid + Tax Advantages

To afford college includes saving on what you pay out on taxes. A business has tax right-offs because of expenses. If you've always wanted to have your own business, you can start small with something right out of your house. The internet is chock-full of ideas of what you can do right now. What follows is what you can save when you hire your children to work in your business. It's a 3-step process:

(1) Establish an unincorporated business, and hire your under-18 year-olds who must be over 6 years of age. Pay them "reasonable wages" (not $50K for filing, but $5K for computer work makes sense to the IRS) even if your business doesn't show a profit. There are no federal withholding income taxes. Work can be full or part-time.

(2) Prove the Deduction Keeping excellent records is a must. Keep a time-sheet and pay your child with a check. The check can be endorsed over to you for deposit into your account to pay for college expenses. It's better that the child's savings be in your account before Dec 31 of the junior year so it's penalized 30% less by the colleges before submitting those complicated financial aid forms.

(3) Give each child a W-2 at the end of the year. And file a tax return. Let's look at an example. You have 2 teenagers under 18. Pay each one up to the maximum standard deduction of $4,750 (in 2006), which means the first $4,750 of income is not taxed. Any extra money earned is taxed at 10%. Check with your accountant first to see how well this works.

Net Result: You paid your children $9,500 ($4,750 X 2) that you can deduct, and it's tax-free to them. If you're in the 20% tax bracket, you saved yourself $1,900 in federal taxes alone; if you're in the 25% bracket, you saved $2,375 in a year.

There can be additional savings. If possible, pay each child an additional $4,000 to be sheltered in a ROTH IRA, keeping in mind that there's a $400 tax. The total savings on each child would now be $8,350 ($4,750 + $4,000 - $400 tax), or $16,700 tax-free. Each child was paid $8,350 tax-free, and the parent gets a deduction of $16,700 with a tax savings of $3,340 (20% tax bracket), or $4,175 (25% tax bracket).

Caution #1: If you've done everything right, there should be no problem. The only issue the IRS could raise is the "reasonableness" of what you paid your child. Work can be any combination of computer work, sweeping floors, filing documents, washing windows, stocking inventory, or making deliveries. The work needs to be evident and preferably on-going. And if the business takes a loss because it's a start-up, you could receive more financial aid because your earnings will be less.

Caution #2: In the above example, the $8,350 earned in the student's senior year will be assessed against the student at 50% above the first $2,500. That's $8,350 minus $2,500 = $5,850 X 50% = $2,925. That's $2,925 which a college will NOT give your child in financial aid that year. But here's the trade-off: the student is still ahead by $5,425 (the other 50% = $2,925 + $2,500). Or, if the student earned $5,000, the loss in aid is $1,250, but your student is still ahead by $3,750. The loss isn't cool, but you've got more money put away, and your child's development of a solid work ethic is a big fat positive for everybody.

Best Kept Secret

Community Colleges

If you're broke, or your child is an under-achiever or totally without radar on his future, or the cost of a 4-year college is prohibitive, take a serious look at a community college. Grades and SATs don't matter; all you need for admission is your checkbook. The costs are much less than either public or private 4-year schools. They account for 1,100 of the more than 4,000 schools in America today. As costs continue to skyrocket, community colleges will become more popular.

The makeup of community colleges closely resembles the small class sizes, the high degree of personal interaction between students, between students and faculty, and a genuine student motivation that are found at small elite liberal arts colleges. These similarities are a parent's dream. As for parents who are distressed about their student's motivation, Dr Thomas E. Gamble, president of Florida's Brevard Community College, says "the community college deals effectively with the student malaise of under-achievers."

A student gave this real-life assessment of the community college experience: "The diversity of the student body, the number of people taking part-time courses, and the lack of residence halls and meal plans (at least at my CC) taught me a lot about self-reliance, money and time management, and removed me from an environment of parties and drinking that would have potentially led me down a path to bad grades and low achievement." This is what every parent would like to read of their student who's attending a 4-year college now.

Admissions directors of high-profile 4-year colleges hold a near universal opinion of these 2-year schools. "Community colleges," says an admissions dean at a Connecticut university, "do a fine job of preparing students to go on to higher education." Instead of being a last resort to higher education, they're effective gateways to higher-level degrees.

From an admissions standpoint, it's easier to be accepted to a 4-year college as a community college transfer than as a high school senior; 33% of applicants to UC Berkeley were accepted from community colleges compared to 28% from high school applicants. Miami Dade College, a community college in Florida with a separate honors program for high-achieving students who aren't ready for the usual 4-year college experience, has agreements with over 50 universities. Nearly half go on to colleges like the University of Wisconsin, Georgia Tech, Cornell, Smith, Yale, and the University of Texas.

The first 2 years of a college education can cost a parent nothing. Here's how it works: the student commutes to a local community college with tuition and books for about $3,500. Add from $500 to $1,000 in transportation expenses, and the total approximates $4,500 a year. The student takes out a Stafford Loan in the first year for $2,650, which the student pays back, not the parent. Plus, a summer job for 15 weeks with a take-home pay of only $150 generates $2,250. So, $4,500 minus the Stafford's $2,650 + the student's $2,250 = $0 out of the parent's pocket.

In the second year, the student qualifies for more money with a Stafford Loan: $3,500. It's another year free of costs for mom and dad. Talk about liberation! You're free of the high costs of college which your friends will pay because they didn't follow the advice you're reading now.

With a game plan to get a degree from a 4-year college, the first 2 years are free to the parents, and the student can qualify for Stafford loans as a transfer student in the junior and senior years of a state school for $5,500 each year. That's another $11,000 parents don't have to pay toward a 4-year degree. In other words, your child can get a 4-year degree from a state school at half the price of other schools, *or less.* Could this be planet earth's easiest no-brainer? It gets better.

Here's the math for a parent's out-of-pocket costs:

- 1st yr of community college: $0 (Stafford pays $2,650 and the student's earnings make up for the smaller balance)

- 2nd yr of community college: $0 (Stafford pays $3,500 and the student's earnings make up for an even smaller balance)
- 3rd yr of 4-year state school in the Northeast (most expensive schools): $16,000 (includes room & board) minus a Stafford Loan of $5,500 = $10,500 out-of-pocket
- 4th yr of 4-year state school in the Northeast: see year 3.

Stafford loans in the 1st year amount to $2,650, and in the 2nd year, $3,500. With a little income-paying job, your student can easily pay the first 2 years of college. Fast-forward to your total out-of-pocket expenditure for a 4-year state school degree: from $10,000 to $21,000. If your student is *commuting in the 3rd and 4th years*, the range in costs could be from $5,000 to $10,000. But here's the mind-blowing secret that allows a parent to pay nothing in the last 2 years:

After reading section, ***Save $30,000 Per Child,*** you'll connect the dots and discover that *you can pay absolutely nothing for your student's 4-year degree*. This is the best kept secret about paying for college. Revealed for the first time. Right here. Now you don't have to read Ben Kaplan's *How To Go To College Almost For Free,* because he says, *"Almost."*

This secret comes with 2 bonuses: (1) in 2 years, you can graduate with an Associates degree with at least a 2.5 GPA and you're *automatically* admitted to an in-state 4-year state school as a junior. States such as Florida, Massachusetts and Wisconsin offer such a program; and (2) proudly you can claim you worked your way through college, made the daily sacrifices that struggling parents make, and demonstrated a maturity, a work ethic, and an achievement that no Harvard graduates can put on their resumes.

You win. And win big.

"Harvard students, like others in many universities, often graduate without the core knowledge one would or should expect. One of [Harvard president] Summers's remedies was to have faculty teach more, especially more overview courses that afford students an introduction to different disciplines. The faculty was resistant. Tenured professors prefer to teach courses that tend to track their research, even their latest book, rather than boning up on introductory material they left behind in graduate school. As a tenured professor responded when asked to teach an introductory art history survey, 'No self-respecting scholar would want to teach such a course.'"

Mortimer B. Zuckerman, Editor-in-Chief,
US News & World Report, 4/10/2006

College Award Letters

Award = The Bill

Colleges write Oscar-winning award letters. Typical is one that offered a student a bank of emotional steroids, designed to pump up his enthusiasm for the school - a grant for $6,000 for the first year. Free bucks. No pay-back. What followed next was a titanic offer to sink the family's finances: over $28,000 in loans in the first year. It was the family's Commencement Exercise in the economic realities of the college game.

In your award letter, look for the words, "work-study." Work-study could be an award that requires no work with lots of reward. See section, ***College Work-Study***.

Look for the amount that none of the grants and loans will cover. You'll be forced to do the math. Argh...that's the cost of attendance, less the aid package = your out-of-pocket costs, or what is known as "unmet need."

Note the conditions to keep what's offered. Is the offer good for 4 years? Or, if your student is one of the 53% of the incoming freshman class this year who will graduate in 5 years, will the aid package be good for all 5 years?

Does the school indicate that a private scholarship is deducted? Some colleges will substitute your scholarship for a loan to lesson your loan liability, but other colleges see scholarships as a gift to themselves, a hidden way for them to save money by awarding you a lesser amount that matches the amount of your scholarship. See section, ***Scholarship Highjacking.***

"Award" is a superbly seductive word that is similar to the word "fee," which local governments use to hide the word "tax." Colleges use words like "award" as part of a vocabulary to win the college game.

Never underestimate a college's trademark ability to exercise creative financing at your expense. You may not even notice it with the feel-good language they use, but it'll be right there in the "award" letter, so obvious you're likely to miss it.

After The Award Letters

Get More Money

Most parents on the seemingly credible but expensive advice of their plumber or hairdresser regard the award letter as a document cast in stone. It's not an award letter, it's a paper sedative to lessen the jolt you're receiving by what is truly the bill. Hopefully you've received more than one award letter, so don't lock on to the letter that offers the most aid, but the letter that has you paying the least out-of-pocket. It's not what you get in financial aid, it's what you keep for your retirement. After all, college is a retirement issue.

Either before you apply, or after receiving all the aid you're going to get, call the school's financial aid office and ask them to walk you through your out-of-pocket costs. Discuss the typical campus expenses, like health insurance fees that are never mentioned in a school's catalog. It'll open your eyes and help you decide which school is most affordable. See section, ***College Money Traps***.

Every spring the tables turn. "April," said T.S. Eliot, "is the cruelest month," not so much for you, but for the schools. Except for the most exclusive colleges and universities, the fate of the nation's colleges is now in the hands of 17- and 18-year olds. It's the colleges' turn to be nervous, waiting to see if they will be accepted or rejected. It's not unusual for a college to mail 6,000 acceptance letters to fill 2,000 slots. That means 4,000 picky and demanding teenagers will reject the school. It's nail-biting, high-stakes academic poker for the colleges, and your student is holding nearly all the cards. Play them to the max, but how?

Appeal. Pleading with cookies, cakes, and food baskets don't work. In a non-threatening manner, simply convey in a letter - never call - that you need more *help*, not more financial aid. Indicate that you have a problem accepting the school's offer because it doesn't meet the amount of aid you need, which may force you to attend another school. Or, the school isn't matching a better offer from another school. Schools may request that you fax another school's better offer before they decide to award you more money, which is why you should apply to 10 colleges to get as many offers as possible.

If you have a better offer, also ask for the maximum Federal Work-Study Award. They'll be surprised that you even know this award exists. Each year thereafter repeat the request. Over 4 years it could mean thousands of dollars in additional financial aid. This is how you win the college game.

Colleges minimize the dollar amount in their "awards" because they're gambling that you'll accept whatever they offer. Unfortunately, they win most of the time because most parents don't appeal, it never crosses their minds. To increase the college's offer, simply ask. For each of our clients we use a creative appeal strategy that glove-fits their circumstances.

The student, never the parent, signs the get-to-the-point, half-page appeal letter. Financial aid officers, many of whom are parents themselves, are more motivated to make you feel better with a little more money than to give you a generous aid package. Moreover, send a copy of your appeal to the admissions director since s/he made the decision to accept your child. There's no guarantee it'll work, but hundreds of my clients are happy with the results. What do you stand to lose if you don't ask? Call me for more details at 1-888-876-1863.

Colleges have an appeal allowance that is never disclosed in college catalogs. It's a college's best public relations hammer to nail down your commitment to help make their April peptic seizures go away. Appeals for more aid are particularly effective with all colleges when there's a recent lay-off of one parent, divorce, or some event that signals an economic hardship in the months ahead. In these cases, documentation will be required, and colleges will use what is known as "Professional Judgment" to make a decision on matters that don't fit their standard formulas. In most cases, families receive more aid. This is a great public relations opportunity for a college, a rare moment where you can witness a college helping you win the college game.

Unless a college has agreed to meet 100% of your need for more money, use the 3-Strikes-And-You're-Out rule: appeal your award until you are denied 3 times. And always send your appeals by Priority Mail with Signature Confirmation, not Return Receipt. To avoid a public relations nightmare, colleges won't revoke your admission just because you were a pest about asking for help. Be a pest and ignore this clever public relations ploy by the colleges: their phone call.

After admitting your student, a college is ready to cozy up. Their phone call is the heart-pounder that declares, "We're family now." *Watch your caller ID and ignore the call.* But if you answer by mistake, and a voice says, "We're awarding your student another two thousand dollars because of your request for help," do *not* express excitement. Respond with a dull "Thank you, but I'd appreciate confirmation in writing." On the other hand, if you hear the college official deny your request for more aid, you can start stumbling and mumbling. No matter what, give the same exact reply. Their call is your signal to begin writing your next appeal letter. The letter should never ask for more money; however, it should ask for more *help*. It's not what you say, it's how you play it.

Lots of acceptance letters increase your chances for more aid. One of my students applied to 14 colleges, but some were on a whim. Within 11 days, a whim college responded with $76,000 in grants to be used over 4 years. She was suddenly in the grips of a Rodney Dangerfield moment: a college responding so fast with so much free money must have made a mistake. But quantity gave her quality: I used the grant letter to leverage more money from the school of her choice, an extra $8,000 to be exact.

A very smart student wasn't so lucky. He applied to only one school. Not very smart. After receiving his acceptance letter, there was one problem: he was forced to take the Mister Scrooge Scholarship, the minimum offered by the school. Though the student got what he wanted, his parents got what they didn't want: a heaving case of heartburn, a full bag of regrets, and a retirement account going south.

"Our student financial aid system supports the 'investment in me' approach by making less money available in the form of grants to needy students, and more in the form of loans to be paid back as a return on the individual's investment in themselves. The message our kids get is that they're not students; they're consumers. And if they're willing to settle for 'purchasing' a degree that means nothing in terms of educational achievement, it's their right. It's their investment. In this environment, professors, colleges, and universities are forced into giving the customers what they want, not necessarily what they *should* want."

John Merrow

If Your Aid Isn't Enough

Try These Alternatives

Some schools, particularly the private colleges and universities, which have large endowments (read: big bucks growing in investments seemingly without purpose), have more flexibility when it comes to your negotiating a better financial aid package. State colleges have very little room to offer anything. Infamous bank robber, Willie Sutton, would remind you to keep your eyes on private schools - that's where the money is. See section, ***Private Colleges.***

Understand all payment options available to you just in case the college your child is dying to go to comes up short when offering you financial aid.

Start At A State School And Then Transfer To A Private College.

If your student gets accepted to both private and state schools, and they prefer to go to one of the private schools, the first thing you need to look at is how much it is really going to cost you to send him/her to that school.

If the private university offers you an excellent package, which makes it approximately the same cost to you as the state school, your decision is fairly easy; however, if the private university offers you a less-than-competitive package, and sending your student there will put you both in serious debt, my recommendation is to send your child to a community college for two years and then transfer. See section, ***Best Kept Secret.***

If your student wants to transfer to a private university and doesn't plan on working for top grades (B+ or better), transferring will be very difficult. Also, schools tend not to offer their best aid packages to transfer students.

Send Your Student To A College That Offers Cooperative Education.

About 900 colleges and universities across the country offer programs that students can alternate between full-time study and a full-time job. This differs from work-study in that work-study jobs tend to be part-time jobs until the amount of the award is earned. Downside: it may take 5 years or more to graduate.

On the upside, cooperative education offers periods of full-time employment in jobs that the student is interested in pursuing after graduation.

Go Military.

There's ROTC (Reserve Officer Training Corps). To qualify for an ROTC Scholarship, which usually covers full or partial tuition plus an allowance of $100/mo, your student must apply in the senior year of high school. Above-average grades and above-average SAT scores are a must.

Apply to one of the military academies. Your student must have top grades and SAT scores, pass a rigid physical, and have a recommendation from a Congressman or Senator. It's a free education if you can meet the high standards, and it'll require a commitment to military service for several years.

Borrow The Money. You considered this already.

Look at federally subsidized loans from a local bank, which are interest-free until your child graduates, and you have 10 years to repay. The parent Plus loan has a fixed interest rate at 8.5%, but the rate doesn't vary. Borrow as much as you need, less what you can afford to pay. Students with bad-credit parents can qualify for more money under the unsubsidized Stafford Loan. See section, ***Save $30,000,*** item #3.

The Signature Student Loan is popular. Your student gets the loan from Sallie Mae, the parent cosigns it, and the student gets to start paying it back with his or her first job. Students have up to 15 years to repay at a minimum of $50 per month.

You can always borrow from your cash-value life insurance policy, or from your mattress account, both tax-free. If possible, borrow from your 401(K) or 403(B). Withdrawing from your retirement account is a last-resort recommendation. Move heaven and earth to avoid taking pre-59½ taxable distributions from your retirement funds. That's because you're penalized three ways: (1) you're taxed on the extra income you have to report; (2) you're taxed on the withdrawal you make; and (3) because you increased your EFC by increasing your income, you qualify for less aid. For every dollar you withdraw from your retirement accounts, it could cost you up to 50 cents on the dollar in lost financial aid. That hurts.

Consider a home equity loan, even a new cash-out refinance of your mortgage, instead of a commercial loan since all of your interest payments, which likely will be less than the government's 8.5%, will be tax-deductible. Since lenders are advertising them to death (well, not quite), home equity loans are very popular.

There's a creative strategy that is virtually unknown to banks, colleges, or financial planners. It's using the equity in your home in conjunction with a MEC to lower your EFC and win BIG in the financial aid game, especially with private colleges. See section, ***Asset Strategies.*** Caution: some college financial planners take a cookie-cutter approach by suggesting you refinance and put the cash-out into a MEC, as if to suggest there's no other way to pay for a college education. Call me to discuss whether or not it fits *your* personal financial situation: 1-888-876-1863.

"As faculties are pressed to do more in various areas it is easier to give good grades than hold students to a higher standard."

George Kuh
Director, Indiana University Center for Postsecondary Research

Attendance

What Every Student Must Know

That most famous and entertaining of American philosophers, Woody Allen, once declared that 80% of life is just showing up. Attending class is no tough requirement. But college students at many colleges get extra credit for attending every class. It's like getting paid extra money for showing up to work everyday. Message to students: learning isn't a priority, but appearances are. Message to parents: higher education is getting lower.

Allen would no doubt agree with this student from the University of North Dakota: "Attend class all the time. You may not think that going to class has anything to do with financial aid, but if you get put on probation, there is a chance that you could have your financial aid revoked. Financial aid is a wonderful thing, don't take it for granted."

US News & World Report

What's Missing In The College Issue?

Conspicuous is the absence of a single sentence on the subject of financial aid. It's like publishing a special issue on new down-sized automobiles in a time of high gasoline prices, but not a word is devoted to each car's fuel economy.

"In the end," concluded collegeconfidential.com, "we've noticed that students and parents start out using the magazine rankings to inform themselves, but in the end these rankings have little overall value in the final selection process. Because of this, we give the U.S. News & World Report rankings a 'B-' for making a big splash at first, with little real, residual value in the final analysis."

How about an "F" for no mention of financial aid?

"...the reading proficiency of college graduates has declined in the past decade...Only 31 percent of college graduates can read a complex book and extrapolate from it. That's not saying much for the remainder."

Federal Study,
National Center for Education Statistics,
Comments by Lois Romano,
Washington Post, 12/25/05

College Work-Study
A Great Opportunity

What is it? Your student can work on or off campus for 10-12 hours a week in the library, book store, cafeteria, study hall, or labs. It's minimum wage and no heavy lifting. It can be as high as $4,500 a year, split equally between 2 semesters. The first $2,250 pays for the award; anything extra is yours to keep. It starts all over again in the second semester.

Work Ethic What's it mean to a college when you request work-study? Due to the fact that college is resume-building time, work-study makes a good impression on potential employers. But for those colleges which give you a work-study program, it may mean they're impressed with your desire to participate in the cost of your own education. How do you make that impression? Do it when you get your award letter and the work-study award is missing. At the time of application, put it in writing to read like this: "I would very much appreciate being considered for work-study since I will bear most of the burden of paying for my education." How many requests do you think a college receives like this? Very few.

If you don't qualify for need-based aid and you're wealthy, make sure that each of the children's accounts has less than $100. Then the student should tell the financial aid office in writing that the parents are requiring you to help pay for your own education. On the other hand, if you ask for work-study when you have $23,000 in your savings account, or your baby-brother's account has $23,000, you will have lost credibility. The folks in the financial aid office will treat your request as the Joke of the Day.

Part of getting into the college of your choice and getting what you want is making a first good impression. As the schools are marketing themselves to you, you must be marketing yourself to them. It's how to win the college game.

Free Money Your child can be last in line to sign up for a work-study program and learn there's no job. For example, he's awarded $1,000 for the first semester. He shows up and discovers that the jobs are all gone. The award is now a non-existent work program that will most likely pay $1,000 anyway. Cool. It's your kid's first experience with welfare. Not cool. But no one argues with the result.

A non-award You show up for the job and discover there are too many students for too few jobs, and they remove the award from your aid package. Now you have to pay back the college the award you were given. This scenario doesn't happen often.

Bad hours There's a real job waiting for you, but your work schedule is conflicting with your class schedule. And there's nothing you can do to change it. So you have to decline the work and pay the money you didn't earn.

Appeal You can appeal this result because the conflict in scheduling wasn't the fault of the student. Believe it or not, you may get some free money because you told the financial aid office, "We were really counting on that money. We purposely listed work-study because our daughter needs to help us pay for her own education. What can you do to help us in this predicament?" Where there are mothers working in financial aid offices, pulling at heart-strings can work. But pull gently with determination.

The 3 Little Pigs of Financial Aid

Will Your Pig Fly?

When the Taxpayer Relief Act of 1997 was passed, Uncle Sam gave a tax credit for college tuition and fee payments. Faster than you could spell g-r-e-e-d, enterprising colleges raised their tuition rates to match the tax breaks. In effect, colleges robbed you of your tax credit - legally. These credits come in the form of 3 little pigs, or, what looks like a big tax break is really a little one.

Pig #1. The Hope Scholarship Credit: You can receive a tax credit (better than a deduction) of up to $1,500 per student for tuition and fees during the student's first 2 years of college. "A tax credit," says the IRS, "reduces the amount of income tax you have to pay. Unlike a deduction, which reduces the amount of income subject to tax, a credit directly reduces the tax itself." This pig has lipstick, which means there's hope for some tax relief, even if it's not the full $1,500.

Pig #2. The Lifetime Learning Credit: You may be able to claim the Lifetime Learning Credit of up to $2,000 for qualified education expenses paid for all students enrolled in eligible post-secondary educational institutions. There is no limit on the number of years the lifetime learning credit can be claimed for each student. **Caution:** It's a credit per tax return, and you can't use it in combination with the Hope Credit. To get the benefit of either credit, your joint incomes cannot exceed $102,000. For higher incomes, try...

Pig #3. The Tuition and Fees Tax Deduction is $4,000 if your adjusted gross income (AGI) is not more than $130,000. If your AGI is over $130,000, but less than $160,000, you only get $2,000 of tax relief. Whatever lipstick you find here disappears when you realize you can't get the full benefit if you take this deduction, and itemize your deductions, or claim more than 3 exemptions.

TIP #1: Take the Hope Scholarship Credit in the first 2 years of college and the Lifetime Learning Credit for the remaining years.

TIP #2: If you didn't file for any of these credits/deductions in the past, ask your accountant if you can file an amended return (1040X) for the applicable year(s) to get money back from the IRS. Chances are good that a little stash of cash is waiting for you.

TIP #3: Ask colleges if they count your tax credit as income. If they do, ask that they drop this penalty. Why? Because the credit was established in the Taxpayer Relief Act to give financial *relief* to parents. But many colleges count this legal credit as added income. It's an immoral excuse to give you less aid. In sum, a college is penalizing you for taking a legitimate, Congressionally-approved, family-helping, deficit-reducing and financially stress-relieving credit. Colleges violate the most basic moral principle of justice. Tell the college that you're simply asking for fairness. The result may be a pleasant surprise since colleges rarely see this complaint. You can win.

Put the colleges on notice that you're not the typical unquestioning parent. Whenever possible, never give a college the slightest control over your money, and at all times, when communicating, be pleasant, but matter-of-fact in your tone.

Your accountant may be intimately familiar with these 3 little pigs, so ask if you qualify. If you don't qualify, you won't be surprised. If you do qualify, at least one pig will fly.

Drive Colleges Crazy

Weaponize Your Money

As many as 70% of accepted students won't show up for the fall semester. Colleges want you to send in your deposit by the usual May 1st deadline in order to guarantee your child a place in the freshman class. That's because the good folks in the admissions office expect to suffer from ESPD, Expected Student Population Disorder. They're nervous about not really knowing the exact number of students who will actually attend, or, that 70% of the students they accept will not attend. Even colleges bite their nails at the prospect of getting rejected by a terrific bunch of 17- and 18-year-olds every May. So what's behind the ESPD that drives the college admission departments crazy?

Multiple depositing. Or, money you weaponize.

After your student has been accepted at several colleges, but can't make up his or her mind which to attend, hedge your bets. Send your top 2 or 3 colleges their required deposit by May 1st to signal that you're coming (but you're not sure yet). You want to make sure there's a place for your student who's been accepted, but s/he needs more time to decide. The colleges want to assume that your deposit represents a guarantee to attend their school. Because they are aware of this practice of multiple deposits, or kids not making up their minds, they're irritated by parents who do it.

Why? Because they claim a parent is buying a slot that prevents someone else from getting it. You've denied someone a place at their university by sending in a deposit that signals you've decided to go there. "Unlike the airlines that don't have to guarantee you a seat," said one dean of admissions, "we have to guarantee you a bed when we receive your deposit." And, lo and behold, your student goes elsewhere. The colleges say this result is an unfair body-blow to the student who lost the slot, as if to suggest that the student who lost also hasn't made multiple deposits. Talk about spin: what the schools are really saying is that multiple depositing is an unfair body-blow to them. Schools would love life to be fair (read: everything on their terms).

You shouldn't care what colleges think. This is your student's future and your hard-earned money that are at stake. In reality the college's focus is not on your kid's future or your money, it's on *their* future and *their* money, not to mention the unknown number of students who are going to show up in September. Colleges constitute a business industry that, like every other business, dislikes the vagaries and uncertainties of the marketplace. It's antacid time at the admissions office. You've discovered another way to win the college game.

Sometimes the schools end up with a few empty rooms, and sometimes they're renting motel rooms. Because admissions and financial aid constitute a game that was devised long ago by the colleges who also made the rules, are parents required to care if the opponent loses? Are you required to feel guilty when your student wins? Don't hold your breath waiting for a college to cheer your victory.

Colleges have a silver lining in their cloud. Because the college game is all about money, they've already factored in, based on past Septembers, the approximate but inexact number of students who will show up. They forget this is not a marriage transaction, but a business decision that parents must make to their own advantage.

Score to win: weaponize your money by making those multiple deposits.

Wait-Listed

It Could Be Profitable

Like an airline standby, you can get on the flight if a seat becomes available. You've been accepted to this college, but not until they've screened everyone else. Welcome to Purgatory University, or college limbo. While you're waiting, the college of your choice is handing out gobs of money to students who applied earlier and/or had better GPAs and/or SATs. How much does that leave for you once you're notified that you can come but maybe much of the money's been allocated already?

Even if your student has a near perfect SAT score, a 4.0 GPA, makes singer-guest appearances with the Los Angeles Symphony, runs a 3-minute mile, and you work 3 jobs to feed your family, you could be passed over by a student with lesser grades, who performed 10 minutes of community service, but whose parents are wealthy. Why? Wealthy parents are the economic heroes to the college that relies on a need-sensitive admissions policy. Money talks and poor students walk. See section, ***2 Dirty Secrets***.

Parents with lots of money save these colleges big bucks because they also make large donations to their multi-million dollar endowment funds. The few but growing mega universities with billion-dollar endowments simply show their true school colors: green and green.

Why would colleges act this way? If you need aid, the college will certainly give you some. That's bad for the college. If you don't need aid because your family has too many assets and your income is too high, colleges don't have to give you any money. That's good for the college. Not qualifying for aid makes it much easier for the college to admit you in a flash. It's the ultimate no-brainer for the college's financial aid office. The waving flag of economic discrimination is flying high on many American college campuses.

Such unfairness works hand-in-hand with acceptable racial discrimination (aka "good racism"). If there are 2 affluent students of equal talent and one has a minority-looking name, is there any doubt who gets admitted? This plays oh-so-conveniently into the school's cosmetic diversity. The college ends up giving itself a two-for-one deal: it saves a bundle of cash, and admitting a minority student validates the school's ongoing self-congratulatory devotion to the gods of political correctness. See section, ***The Cost Of Diversity.***

What's your solution? Have an agreement with your child that you will place the college on *your* waiting list. If your student is later accepted, wait for the usual follow-up award letter. If the wait-listed school (even if it's not your first choice) offers more financial aid than those schools that accepted your student, use their letter as leverage to get more aid out of your first choice. To be wait-listed could be profitable.

Attitude check: because of the multitude of colleges to choose from, you don't need the college. In effect, allow yourself to maintain some control of the admissions process instead of surrendering it to a college. Part of your admissions strategy must include the practicality of choosing several other schools where the student can be happy. Top students should see section, ***The Math Of Admission.***

Warning to your student: don't overdose on why you want to go to a particular college, only to ignore more than 4,000 other choices. Why would you allow any college to force your parents to pay top dollar and *burden yourself with more debt after graduation?* That would make losers of you both.

Once you have made your final decision on which college to attend, I urge you to contact all the schools that accepted your student and tell them your child isn't coming so that a wait-listed student can have your slot. It could mean someone's hopes being realized and their dreams fulfilled. It's the right thing to do.

Cheaper In Canada

Not Found In US News & World Report

In the movie, *Goodbye Girl*, financially-strapped Richard Dreyfuss wanted to make a great impression on a first date. Before knocking on her door, he walked into a liquor store and blurted out, "Give me the best, cheapest wine you've got!" Some parents have been very impressed to discover that some of the best, cheapest colleges are found in Canada. With its own best schools, the cost can be 1/2 the price of US schools. Here are 3 good examples:

University of Toronto Rated the #1 school in Canada. Its cost in US dollars approximates $23,000-$25,000 a year with single room and meal plan. America's top-rated colleges cost between $45,000 and $50,000 a year. The U of T has had "major research achievements such as the discovery of insulin, the creation of the first electronic heart pacemaker, the single lung transplant and the discovery of the gene responsible for the most severe form of Alzheimer's disease." Morley Safer of *60 Minutes* claims Toronto to be the best-designed city in North America. Flight time from Boston to Toronto: 1 hr 38 min; Drive time from Boston, MA to Ithaca College (NY): 6 hrs 30 min. See **Free Travel** on the next page.

Univ of Toronto website: http://www.utoronto.ca

McGill University is an English-language university located in the center of one the largest French-speaking cities in the world. A modern city with a distinctly European flair, Montreal is home for one of Canada's largest universities with almost 30,000 students, offering programs in some 300 disciplines. Cost in US dollars per year: $22,000-$24,000 with a single room and meal plan. This school may be the best bargain in all of North America. Flight time from Boston to Montreal: 1 hr 10 min; Drive Time from Boston, MA to Univ of Vermont, 4 hours 36 min

McGill University website: http://www.mcgill.ca

Dalhousie University Located in the heart of eastern Canada's most popular tourist city, Halifax, Nova Scotia. Dalhousie's campus is within walking distance of other colleges, historic sites, and seaside attractions. Students come from all across Canada and over 100 countries. A number of Dalhousie's departments have been ranked among the best in the country. Cost in US dollars: $15,000-17,000/yr with a single room and meal plan. Flight time from Boston to Halifax: 1 hr 25 min; Drive Time from Boston, MA to Villanova (PA): 5 hr 34 min

Dalhousie University website: http://www.dal.ca

Free Travel With higher gasoline prices, you can fly FREE to and from these schools if you get one of those airline credit cards. They allow you to earn bonus miles on purchases made at gas stations, supermarkets, home improvement and hardware stores, drugstores, U.S. Post Office, and how about this? - paying for college! You'll feel right at home when these colleges have you fill out the standard FAFSA form for financial aid.

It's a good time to look north of the border. It's a proven way to win the college game.

Outside The Mainstream

Special Groups Get Help

Separated or Divorced Parents

If you're currently divorced or separated, and your child will be applying to college, consider:

1. The financial aid forms should be completed by the parent with whom the student lives for 6 months and one day of the year. For example, if a child lives with his mother for 9 months out of the year and with his father only 3 months, the income and asset information should be based on the mother only.

2. If the parent with whom the child resides is remarried, you must include the income and the assets of the stepparent as if he or she was the biological parent. This may not sound fair, but this is the way the financial aid formulas work.

3. Private colleges and universities can ask to see the income and asset information of the "other" divorced parent when awarding their own funds. However, this information will not affect federally-based funds.

Although most financial aid is based on "need," financial aid packages are based to some extent on how much colleges want your child. There are 3 "special interest" groups:

Academic Superstars Many schools try to attract top students away from the more highly-rated schools by offering academic scholarships. If your child is academically gifted, use this as a bargaining chip. This is how millionaires with talented kids get FREE money.

Athletes Division #2 or #3 schools offer preferential packaging (more grants, less loans) to attract your child to their school even if s/he is not qualified for Division #1. Meet the coach at each school you visit. Get the high school coach to write letters of recommendation to Division 1 schools, and have the coach contact the college's coach to brag about your student.

Minorities Find out about the availability of scholarship programs for minorities. There's debate over awarding these types of scholarships, but colleges in several states currently have these types of awards.

Owning Your Own Business If you currently own your own business, or you're thinking of starting one, there are significant benefits when it comes to getting money for college. For example, business assets are counted much less heavily than personal assets. Also, you have the ability to control (or lower) your income during the years that your child is in college, thereby making you eligible for more financial aid. See section, ***Start A Business Now.***

Recently Unemployed If you were recently terminated, or have received notice that you will be terminated, or if you own your own business and cannot make a living due to current economic conditions, you must make the college financial aid officer aware of this immediately.

For special circumstances there is something called "Professional Judgment" that a financial aid officer can use to help you out in tough situations. To request it can be very productive.

Independent Students Six criteria determine independent status:

1. twenty-four years of age or older before Dec 31st of their first year of college;
2. armed forces vet;
3. an orphan or ward of the court;
4. have legal dependents;
5. a graduate or professional student;
6. married.

If your child doesn't fit into one of the above criteria, your request for financial aid probably won't fly. But here's where it will fly...

Illegal Aliens This in-your-face phenomenon drives my clients bonkers. Currently 8 states are violating federal law (Title 8, Chapter 14, Sec 1623 of the US Code) by allowing the same in-state fees at state schools for the students of illegal aliens. If you're an American-born parent who speaks English, works hard, obeys the law and pays taxes, and your child attends a state school that's out-of-state, an illegal alien could easily enjoy paying half of your rate. Here are the states where out-of-country, non-citizen, and legal-age law-breakers get a big break on tuition fees at USA state schools from tax-paying and born-in-the-USA citizens: Texas, New York, California, Washington, Utah, Oklahoma, Illinois, and Kansas.

Crime pays for law-breakers in law-breaking states.

"How can anyone rationally argue that a baseball player should get a college scholarship, but a piano player shouldn't? What does it say about a college's regard for art, literature, drama and music if the finest young painters, writers, actors and musicians are not eligible for the same rewards as are athletes?"

Frank Deford,
Senior Writer, Sports Illustrated

How Students Flunk IN

Is Flunking Out A Thing Of The Past?

Ever hear of a college student flunking OUT of a $40,000-a-year college? No? Ever wonder why? Because the student's parents are an ATM machine: it empties the parents' required amount into the school's coffers every month like clockwork. What financial institution would mess with success?

If your student is doing badly from your perspective, you can rest assured that the college has a different point of view. It's not likely to shut you down. That's called Flunking IN. Your student gets to stay IN school. And you get to marvel at the school's generosity of tolerance for underachievers. Or, you've resigned yourself to the reality that there's no such thing as "educational malpractice."

"And it's not just the colleges that are implicated in this," says Patrick M. Callan, President of the National Center for Public Policy & Higher Education. "Most states fund higher education based on how many students they enroll. So if a student drops out, and they can put another one in that seat the next day or the next quarter, there's no consequence for the college, in terms of the public accountability."

If your student doesn't get the grades to justify your expense, they can marvel at your intolerance for mediocrity or failure. Then it's time to transfer to the school of hard knocks, where your child can live the joy of repeating over fifty times a day, "Would you like fries with that?"

When my first offspring decided not to attend an art class and received an F grade, he remembers my warning him that a repetition of an F grade meant my helping him pack his bags and coming home for good. I made it crystal clear that there was no such thing as a parental subsidy for failure. To this day he declares that it was the most motivating email he ever read in college. It was my own version of flunking IN, the only version I recommend.

"What remains of the '60s on our campuses are its worst sides: intolerance of dissent,...the self-appointed power...to set everyone else's moral agenda, and, saddest of all, the belief that universities not only may but should suspend the rights of some in order to transform students, the culture, and the nation according to their ideological vision and desire."

Alan Charles Kors & Harvey A. Silverglate,
The Shadow University, from the Introduction

College Money Traps
After Your Student Shows Up

To get more of your money in the college game, colleges and universities are like mosquitoes at a backyard barbecue: they'll nickel-and-dime you to distraction, especially if your child's a 1st-year student. The following examples say it all:

1. Paper & Parking Copies from an ordinary copy machine can cost 15 cents a page (U Connecticut) when a typical print shop charges less. My son can purchase $450 worth of books for his next semester for $190 on the internet, but college bookstores happily charge full price. Pay a $10 fine for the first time you're caught without a parking sticker; $30 for the third time; or, $50 for the fifth time (U Massachusetts). Parking violations are such a big business that colleges relish the thought of having hundreds of 1st-year students with cars on campus.

2. Lost & Late Pay $25 to replace your lost student ID (Fitchburg State College). A late book return to the library, after a grace period, can mean a fine of $25 per book per day (Boston College). Late decisions on course selections can cost $25 (U New Hampshire). If you're late in dropping a class after a deadline, it can cost you $600 (Worcester State College). Or, a private college will still charge you the full semester's tuition - with no refund - if you drop a course whose pro-rated value is $3,000 (Holy Cross). Watch $35 fly out of your wallet when you replace your room key (Clark U).

3. Picky & Petty Your student checks out a computer from the computer lab. Not noticing that anything is missing, the computer is returned without its canvas case. Your student is hit quickly with the meaning of a 20-dollar deficit. But there was no canvas case in the first place. There was no record signed as to the condition of the borrowed item. You lose. Or, each of the library computers has a small sticker that notifies the user not to use the computer for email. If caught, you're fined. Watch those hardly-noticeable installment fees - could be 1.5% of your total. Or, the extra $500 for health insurance you don't need. Here's a nightmare from one student: "I didn't realize that if I dropped a class after the

5th instructional day it would count toward termination of my financial aid."

Colleges hide behind the firewall that protects them from the most stressed bill-payers - parents - who do not have to be notified about what the student forgets, or ignores. Instead, being of legal age, it's the student's responsibility (read: Because students pay little or no attention, the parents will pay). If the student is a freshman, that's when the parent is most vulnerable. Your freshman may have this mindset: "Rules? What rules?!" Eighteen year-olds, away from controlling parents for the first time, are easily tempted to ignore rules. Because this fact is life-sustaining oxygen to the colleges, they carefully set their profit-center traps and place them all over campus. Sooner or later, your student will step in one. Ka-ching!

When does it end? Never. The so-called "real world" started the day your student showed up. To add insult to injury, colleges don't wait for your student to graduate: they want contributions from you now. Like death and taxes, solicitations are guaranteed until death. Even after death.

What to do? Both parent and student should have a copy of the college's calendar of deadlines and campus rule book. They are the gold standards used by the colleges to get your gold. Write personal letters with documentation to reverse unreasonable fee charges. Read your bills carefully - mistakes happen. Most of all, with patience, be a real pain.

Don't bother reminding the college of the most sacred rule in marketing: the customer is always right. They don't believe it for a second.

6 Survival Tips

First 6 Weeks Of College

My clients with entering college freshman receive this masterpiece of tips. More college freshmen will drop out of college in the first 6 weeks than at any other time this year (53% will drop out after the first year). But the 6 tips below have proven to work, according to Dr. R. Gilbert of Montclair State University in New Jersey:

1. Treat your roommates like they're your best friends...even if they aren't.

2. Never assume anything...no matter what your question. Keep asking until 2 people give you the same exact answer.

3. No matter what your problem...there is an expert on campus to help you. First, check with your Head of Residence. Then, go to the Dean of Students office.

4. Don't be intimidated. College *looks* much more difficult than it really is.

5. When you think everyone else is so much smarter than you, remember this quote: "College is a fountain of knowledge. A few come to drink, a few come to sip, and, unfortunately, the rest come to gargle."

6. When you feel like dropping out, repeat slowly this question several times:

"Would you like fries with that?"

This last one gets a chuckle, but it's no joke. Like the condemned man about to be executed, it forces a student to focus on what's really important.

"...we are finding that grade inflation is... symptomatic of a larger problem which someone described as 'a mutual non-aggression pact' between teacher and student: don't ask much of me, and I won't ask much of you."

John Merrow

Why Pay An Expert?

A National Group's Big Bamboozle

An experienced financial aid specialist knows where the college's gold is hidden, and smart parents know it's worth paying an expert to get some of it. Private colleges don't fear that you're going to hire someone who finds the gold. Why? Because these experts are so few and hard to find, which means very few parents will use them. And besides, colleges are too arrogant to care.

But financial aid administrators who have their own organization, the National Association of Student Financial Aid Administrators, want to warn you about these experts. It's the classic story of the elephant fearing the mouse. Since an administrator's expertise is a one-note song telling you how and where to get more loans to afford college, here's their never-ending mantra, their unabashed advisory statement on their website (www.nasfaa.org) as of this writing: "Before considering a consultant, first speak to a financial aid administrator."

It's the equivalent of suggesting that, should you need your car engine repaired, you should go to a young kid who only pumps gas, instead of speaking to an experienced mechanic at the same service station. In other words, this group would have you believe that both occupations are equivalent, one is as good as the other, and that both can perform the same functions. Even though both are in the same work area, their areas of expertise are worlds apart. This group can't resist barking: "A financial aid administrator can perform these same services [of a consultant] free of charge."

Same services? What we have is this group's...

Big Bamboozle They list 5 functions that suggest a match to exactly what they do: preparing the FAFSA, estimating your resources, your EFC, your financial need, and "the types of federal, state, local and institutional aid programs that are available." But they don't perform 4 out of the 5 functions themselves. They only perform the 5th function: their purpose is to describe "the types of federal, state, local and institutional aid programs that are available." They do a good job of it. But it would appear that they want you to believe the list they contrived is all we experts do. It's not a "misstatement," not a "false statement," but a bamboozle.

Financial Aid Experts There aren't enough of them, and this association would have you think that the experts are kids at the gas pump. Experts do more than paperwork; they provide valuable information on how to appropriate aid from colleges for families who qualify for aid, and how to use tax-favored devices to afford college for families who don't qualify for need-based aid. Parents and students have saved thousands of dollars with such information, and have gladly paid for it. Financial aid administrators won't accept that they are the kids at the pump, and their website's whoppers do an enormous injustice not only to this tiny group of experts, but more importantly to the financially-burdened parents who need and want them.

The Math Of Admission

Where To Get Accepted

Know exactly where to apply by finding out your chances of admission.

Why do Harvard and Yale reject over 92% of the best and brightest applicants? Why is any multi-talented and academically-gifted student turned down by an exclusive college or university? It's because there's a mismatch. It's that simple. Unless your student meets a predetermined profile of what the college is looking for in their next freshman class, you're toast.

I found a company that has the ability to predict a top student's chances for admission to any one of the 150 best undergraduate colleges, and they do it with a 98.2% accuracy rate that comes with a money-back guarantee. After speaking with the enterprising co-founder of the company, Matt Schuldt, who attended Princeton University and later received his MBA from Dartmouth's Tuck School of Business, I was impressed enough to offer the company's services to my clients. When asked what's behind his company's accuracy rate, his reply:

"Our experts have developed unique statistical algorithms for each college that compare a student's background and achievements to the college's numerous admissions criteria including standardized test scores, extracurricular activities, academic record, background and more."

The company stays in constant contact with admissions departments of the top schools to get each of their criteria for selection for the next school year. For example, the freshmen at Duke University in 2002 were given preference based on their race, residency, legacy status, athletic prowess and parent-donor status. This is why valedictorians were rejected - they simply didn't meet this school's particular criteria for that year.

Getting the best grades and the best test scores are the required start in the right direction, but as I've stated all through this book, there's a lot more that goes into the decision to admit your child, even if you don't like what you've discovered in the section, ***The Cost Of Diversity***. On the positive side, your student's achievements and background could very well match better schools that you haven't even considered.

Now you can choose and predict which colleges your high-achieving student has a chance of attending. Statistical data and quantitative analysis are used to accurately match your student to the colleges to which they *should* or should *not* apply, and as an added benefit, it'll save you the expense and time of applying and visiting colleges that won't match. Guess work, parent and student emotions, guidance counselor bias, and your hairdresser's advice are all replaced by an objective template.

To discover where your top student has the best chance of getting into the best colleges, go to this website:

www.go4college.com

As of this writing, I have an access code that will give you a discount to the site's already published rate. If you would like the free code number, email me your request at

p.hemphill@comcast.net

What You Absolutely Must Do Now...

Student: To Get Into The College Of Your Choice...

1. **Get a study *attitude*** by repeating this statement: "I succeed because I love learning." Say it to yourself every chance you get. Post it so you can see it often. Your level of success will depend on the *intensity* of your *belief* in what you're repeating. Read the last sentence again. Start your winning attitude now. And don't stop.

2. **Get a study *habit*** by studying in 20-minute segments, followed by a 5-minute break. After 20 minutes, stand up and move around. Go back for another 20 minutes and continue the pattern until you have *mastered,* or completed your assignment. During the breaks, enjoy an activity, or get some fresh air. Breaking up your time also avoids getting bored. This pattern will get you better grades. If you repeat what I suggested enough times and commit yourself to this pattern, better grades are in your future. Keep your attitude positive, and avoid negative people.

3. **Go to www.myroad.com.** It'll help you find out who you are. This site will help you discover what you want to major in before you go to college, and what colleges will be a fit for you.

4. **Go to www.dosomething.org.** Find just ONE thing you'd love to do, and continue doing this ONE thing all through high school; this website will help you find what kind of community project fits you. When colleges see that you have a passion for *something*, and you get good grades, they'll practically beg you to attend their school. They do it by giving you scholarships and grant money! How cool is that? By having a good study ***attitude*** and a study ***habit***, you'll succeed!

Parent: To Pay For College

1. Encourage your student with what's on the previous page. (Note that I made this # 1)

2. Read and review this book thoroughly.

3. Look at your finances. If you have none to speak of - no stocks, bonds, mutual funds, CDs, gold, jewelry, retirement funds, mattress money, and piggy banks - you may qualify for lots of financial aid. But you need to know how to maximize your eligibility.

4. If you have assets (don't count money that's already in your retirement), you need to reposition them now. Not next month, but now. Act with a sense of urgency. Most people mistakenly call me the last minute. But if your student is already in high school - *regardless of grade* - you need to take action now.

5. Call me for a free consultation: 1-888-876-1863.

Acknowledgements

Perhaps the most conscientious person with whom I have ever had the honor of working, who is passionate about helping my clients and always rises to the occasion where most would fail, even when it means helping a frantic parent with a FAFSA form question or a worried student with an application detail, on a weekend or late at night, I'm pleased to salute Amy Eagle. Her infectious sense of humor and feedback on this work has been rewarding for me and, I must say, a lot of fun.

Thanks to Dr. George R. Boggs, President and CEO of the American Association of Community Colleges, I was able to make some slight but necessary adjustments to the section, ***Best Kept Secret***.

Michael Thomas, a director on the Alumni Board of Directors of the oldest public high school in America, Boston English High School, did his Harvard class proud with recommendations that improved the manuscript, and whose real estate expertise has done wonders for my clients on how to use home equity to pay for college.

With over 20 years experience as a college admissions director, and a member of the National Association of Admissions Officers, Nancy Parchesky of Franklin, MA was helpful is clarifying some of my own perceptions and research of the admissions process.

Dan Maga, who owns his own financial planning firm near Chicago, has been very informative regarding the financial issues that are found in this book, and he's an impressive advisor whose clients know he's there when they need him.

Jeffrey Morand, of JP Morand in Englewood, Colorado, who was gracious enough to write the Forward, is tireless in his efforts to provide his clients with the most up-to-date information to better their financial situation, particularly in the area of college costs.

Then there's the energetic professor, Ron Caruthers of Carlsbad, California, who makes me wish I were back in college just to have him as a teacher. Ron's enthusiasm is contagious, and financial aid experts, let alone his own customers, are inspired every time he speaks about his favorite subject.

Finally, my wife, Ann Marie, was understanding of my efforts to help "my students," as I like to call them, and remained most supportive of seeing this book through to its completion.

Article Sources

Introduction: A Warning Alan M. Dershowitz's interview on the Hugh Hewitt radio show, transcript published on www.hughhewitt.com, 2/25/06; "Families are stretching even more to attend a public four-year college...spending 21 percent of their income. Private colleges are the most expensive, requiring that families spend a stunning 33 percent of their income." *Paying for College: The Rising Cost of Higher Education,* MassINC study by B. T. Long, Dana Ansel and Greg Leiserson, 4/06; "Over half of students graduating from four-year colleges in the U. S. lack the literacy to deal with such 'real life' tasks as understanding newspaper editorials, comparing credit card offers, or summarizing the results of a survey,"..."Nor do they have the math skills needed to balance their checkbooks, according to a new study by the Pew Charitable Trusts." *Cash $trapped Colleges*, quoting David Schaefer of Holy Cross College, The Conservative Voice, Malcolm A. Kline, 4/30/06; The Ivy League mindset may be summarized by this question from Richard Baehr, The American Thinker blog, *The College Rejection Bonanza,* 4/7/06: "So why are the elite schools able to take so much pleasure in delivering unprecedented quantities of bad news?" He offers six answers to the question; for insight into what the Ivies think of themselves, the president of Brown welcomed the new freshman class: "You are the smartest, the cutest, the savviest, most dynamic, extraordinary -- I could go on and on." Wall Street Journal, 5/1/06; in his LA Times op-ed piece (4/13/06), *Higher Education: The Status Game,* the president of Colby College admits: "Our students and their parents want to hear--and are told--that they are several cuts above the pack." Apparently, a function of our elitist schools is to plant early the seeds of narcissism and self-absorption; an honest assessment of tuition increases comes from a non-elitist college president, Daniel S. Cheever, Jr., *Is College Worth the Money?* Boston Globe, 6/3/05: "What never seems to end for students and parents, however, is understandable anxiety over paying for college. The relentless rise in the costs of higher education alarms payers and the public." With some urgency, he cautions fellow academics: "College officials must take this issue more seriously." But will they? With brazen sarcasm, the president of Johns Hopkins University made no effort to assuage parental concerns about costs: "Why not reconfigure the Homewood campus into a college for seniors — those over 65 who want to go back and experience the college life perhaps they never had? The golden years group will not be as concerned about tuition costs." *Expensive Tuition? Take Some Tips from Corporate America - Relocate to Cozumel,* William R. Brody, Baltimore Business Journal, 2/27/04; for a scathing critique of college professors, see Al Doyle's *The Biggest Con Game in America,* lewrockwell.com, 5/31/05; here's how an elitist college official responds to counselors who help students get into college and parents save money: "The counseling isn't worth it...Nauseous doesn't begin to describe my reaction...it's a vile, vulgar, cynical rip-off..."

College-Admissions Boot Camp for $10,000 Draws Educators' Ire, Brian Sullivan and Liz Willen, Bloomberg.com, 5/20/05.

Economics 101 Quote from the admissions director of Purdue Univ, US News & World Report, 8/29/05, p 66.

Save $30,000 Per Child *How To Cut College Costs*, A.M. Chaker, Wall Street Journal, 7/15/05; "For low-income and minority students, graduation rates are even worse." "More than 25 percent of college freshmen have to take remedial courses in basic reading, writing, or math..." Kevin Carey, *The Wrong Conversation*, Insidehighered.com, 3/16/06.

2 Dirty Secrets "To help make a Fairfield University education more affordable, administrators there are raising tuition and room and board next year by close to 6 percent. No, really...a freshman biology major at Fairfield U., questions the logic." *Fairfield U., SHU more costly,* L.C. Lambeck, Connecticut Post Online, 5/2/05; CNN Money, Sarah Max, 5/3/05; Associated Press: *Univ of Washington Considers High Tuition-High Aid Model*, 9/2/05; Alan Finder, *Aid Lets Smaller Colleges Ask, "Why Pay for Ivy League Retail?"* NY Times, 1/1/06; 2005 NACUBO Endowment Study, see www.nacubo.org/pressroom; *US bid to keep tabs on tuition irks colleges,* Boston Globe, 7/16/05: "'When the federal government is spending tens of billions of dollars on higher education, and we're asking for a little accountability, then there's no reason why these schools can't provide us with information about why their tuition and fees are increasing,' said...a spokesman for Representative Buck McKeon...." "Despite what they see as statistical shortcomings, some [college] administrators do fear that an unfavorable index could hurt a college's image in a competitive market." Translation: exposing a college's value-for-money-spent formula could prove damaging; a former Brown University admissions director "found the 'quintessential diamond in the rough' -- a black student who had previously not considered a school like Brown." *Building Diversity,* Daily Pennsylvanian, Deena Greenberg, 4/11/06; the hypocrisy of elite colleges may be tied to the QuestBridge College Match program, which in 2005 matched only *46 low-income students* in the nation with full 4-year scholarships to some of the nation's best colleges. See www.questbridge.org; note the title of this Ivy League newspaper article, *Colleges vie for low-income students*, and its self-serving conclusion: "From kindergarten on, [lower-income students] are less likely to attend good schools. Their parents are less likely to have a college education that might help them chart a path to the Ivy League. They do not have access to the SAT coaching, the summer programs or the advising services that have all become staples of the college search for wealthy families." Yale Daily News, 4/27/06; "Some specialists also blame private universities' practice of using a chunk of limited financial aid funds for merit scholarships so they can enroll the most attractive students regardless of whether those students need help. That leaves less money for those who simply need the aid." Boston Globe, 5/1/06; "Church officials said that multiple real estate developers expressed interest in the land, but that Boston College won the bidding because, with its $1.15 billion endowment, the Jesuit university is able to pay cash up front..." *Diocesan headquarters sold to BC*, Boston Globe, 4/21/04; a BC spokesman was asked about the 2006 tuition increase: "Excellence is an expensive proposition," and added that "... spiraling energy costs, and the increasing cost of health insurance for BC employees were also reasons for the increase." The Heights, 4/6/06; when its president, Rev. William Leahy, was asked if BC would ever stop raising tuition, his response was not a sympathy plea to paying parents: "A billion dollars is a great amount of money, but it by no means eliminates all the pressure." Associated Press, Justin Pope, 5/22/05; a college whose endowment (cash stash) exceeds $540,000,000 responded to an aid request from a high-achieving student from a struggling family: "We have reviewed your letter requesting additional financial aid from Northeastern University. We acknowledge that your circumstances are compelling; however, we feel your current award reflects our best effort to reduce your financial burden." Copy of response is in this author's possession; in the most dramatic display of illogical behavior, not uncommon on American college campuses, Yale University admitted a former official of the brutal Taliban regime and defender of the torture of women, but rejected 19,000 innocent applicants in 2006, *Yale Undergrads: The Best, The Brightest, The Taliban?* Janet McMonagle, www.families.com, 5/6/06.

Ask Tough Questions WashingtonSquareNews, 4/13/05; Hubert Herry's article in the NY Times, 4/17/05; *Prospies weigh College's cost in decision,* "...gifted middle-class students must weigh whether attending a top-tier college like Dartmouth is worth the loans their parents will be taking out for that name brand to adorn their sweatshirts and eventually their college diplomas." Dartmouth Online, 4/22/05; Boston Globe, *College: Beyond the Pricetag*, 8/8/05; Dr. Ron Melcher's post on www.carnegiefoundation.org, 5/27/05, 2:22:39 pm; *The College Rejection Bonanza*, Richard Baehr, The American Thinker, 4/7/06; *Saying 'No Thanks' to the Ivy League*: "Even as the price of attending an elite college approaches $50,000 a year, less-prestigious schools are offering more merit aid, making the cost differences starker." Robert Tomsho, Wall Street Journal, 4/24/06; *Estimating the Pay-Off to Attending a More Selective College: An Application of Selection on Observables and Unobservables*, Dale, Stacy Berg and Alan B. Krueger, National Bureau of Economic Research, Inc., 1999; other researchers came to the opposite conclusion, finding that "even after controlling for selection effects, there is strong evidence of significant economic return to attending an elite private institution." See Brewer, Dominic J., Eric R. Eide and Ronald G. Ehrenberg, *Does It Pay To Attend An Elite Private College? A Cross-Cohort Evidence On The Effects Of College Type On Earnings,* Journal of Human Resources, 1999, vol 34, pp 104-123. This is another way academics demonstrate that for every action there's an equal and opposite reaction. Reality: we all deal with the hand we've been dealt with no regrets that we didn't attend an Ivy League school.

The 4-Letter Word Quote from a student aid office appeared in The Bowdoin Orient online, 9/16/05; the quote referring to the new décor of a financial aid office, Boston Globe, 3/20/05; for an equally boneheaded remark from another elitist college in Maine: "But [the dean] recognizes the $55 application fee is an obstacle and a financial burden for some students,..." Let's see if you get this: you're applying to a college whose cost of attendance exceeds $45,000 a year, and a dean says prospective students regard $55 as "an obstacle and a financial burden." Either he's smoking something odd, or you're the type who can't justify buying the house of your dreams because you find the cost of the doorbell "an obstacle and a burden." *Colby College Waives Application Fee for Maine Students*, press release, 8/18/05.

The Cost Of Diversity The US Supreme Court ruled in 2003 that race can be used as a factor in college admissions (Grutter v. Bollinger through compliance with Regents of Univ. of CA v. Bakke); "In the name of diversity, the academic elites have encouraged immigrants to maintain their birth-country cultures and to adopt a stance of separatism and pugnacious victimization." *Sentiment Against Illegals Is Powerful & Growing,* John Leo, RealClearPolitics website, 5/7/06; *Parent Trap*, David Epstein www.insidehighered.com, 7/6/05; *No More Cheating For A Good Cause*, David Gelernter, LA Times, 7/22/05; *College Faculties A Most Liberal Lot,* Howard Kurtz, Washington Post, 3/29/05; *Colorblind Merit has no merit for University of California*, Thomas Lifson, American Thinker blog, 7/15/05; *Why Does College Cost So Much?,* Richard Vedder, Wall Street Journal, 8/23/05; The federal law being broken by 8 states (NY, CA, WA, TX, UT, OK, IL, KS) is Title 8, Chapter 14, Sec. 1623, which states, "an alien who is not lawfully present in the United States shall not be eligible on the basis of residence within a State...for any postsecondary education benefit unless a citizen or national of the United States is eligible for such a benefit." *The Left University: How to Overcome It*, James Piereson, Weekly Standard, 10/03/05; *The College Gender Shift*, Howard and Matthew Greene, Knight Ridder/Tribune News Service, 3/24/04; *A Herd of Academic Minds*, Ed Feulner, Washington Times website, 11/7/05; *Slurring Bush at the New York Times*, Richard Baehr, American Thinker Blog, 5/23/05; *To All The Girls I've Rejected*, Jennifer D. Britz, NY Times, 3/23/06; *Survey reveals pervasive political pressure in the classroom*, American Council of Trustees and Alumni press release, 11/30/04; Thomas Sowell, *College Brainwashing*, RealClearPolitics website, 3/14/06; Oregon State University's "conservative student newspaper, The Liberty, exists on $4,000 a year in private contributions compared to the half a million dollars that the student government spends on a panoply of gay, feminist and environmental groups." *Conservative Student Backlash*, Malcolm A. Kline, The Conservative Voice, 2/17/06; for one school's rationale for discrimination, see Harvard Univ Gazette online

(4/6/06): "A significant number of other incoming students will also bring an international perspective..."; "Yale University enrolls a former Taliban official with a 4th grade education into a non-degree program in the name of diversity, while the University of California attempts to discriminate against students educated at Christian high schools. DePaul University repeatedly makes war on the free speech rights of conservative students and faculty. Stanford University and the College of the Holy Cross attempt to silence the powerful independent voices of their respective established alternative newspapers. On the fourth anniversary of 9/11, Canisius College tries to avoid commemorating the victims, while the University of Iowa opts to hold a 'Peacefest', inviting numerous radical groups including socialists and pacifists, instead of honoring the victims of the national tragedy. Diversity run amok, suppression of free speech, and discrimination against Christians, conservatives, and patriots continue to be the norm in American higher education, and the Collegiate Network (CN) has once again chronicled the worst of those abuses in its 9th Annual Campus Outrage Awards." *2006 Campus Outrage Awards,* www.campusmagazine.org, 4/3/06.

How & Where To Get Free Money, Ball State University's and Stonehill's grant-to-loan ratios, www.collegeboard.com, 5/11/06.

Bad Advice Michael Abernethy, *College education costs rising more and more*, Free Press, Kingston, NC, 8/14/05; Washington Post article by Albert Crenshaw, 8/16/05; *Increase your odds on college aid,* Candace Bahr, www.NCTimes.com, 8/17/05; *Don't hurt yourself when seeking college aid*, R. Shaffer, Boston Herald, 10/9/05; stats on projected costs at state schools from the American Association of State Colleges and Universities, 2004-2005; *Learning the college financial aid system*, A. M. Chaker, Wall Street Journal, 3/28/06.

Before The Junior Year *To All The Girls I've Rejected*, J. D. Britz, NY Times, 3/23/06; see www.go4college.com on how to minimize rejection - or maximize acceptance - at the top 150 schools; "The extra something—a passion or commitment communicated in a clear voice—is what many admissions counselors at top schools say they are looking for." "I think we're all looking for kids who are committed to something, extracurricularly, intellectually, and hopefully both." Brown University dean's comments in the Wall Street Journal, *Who Got Into College?* 4/13/06; "No extracurricular activity experience can take the place of good grades earned in a college-preparatory curriculum." Duquesne University's Paul Cukanna, *Who Gets In? College Admission Officials Offer Their Advice On College Admissions*, Pittsburg-Post Gazette, 2/15/06.

Your College Application *Lying and Deception*, Paul Ekman, Memory For Everyday and Emotional Events, Ornstein & Tversky, Lawrence Erlbaum Publishers, NJ, 1997; Aresty, pp. 65-66; "Anyone can say that you need to have good grades and good standardized test scores to get into college. That is a given. If you find that you are an average student in terms of GPA and standardized testing performance, I have found that there is one little word that can make the difference between being accepted to a university, being put on the waiting list, and being denied admission: Presentation." "In the age of the online application, following very simple rules can separate your application from those of other students. Make sure that your application is neatly presented." "Just because many online applications are free does not mean that you should be nonchalant about how you fill it out. These tips may sound too simple, but you'd be astounded to see how many students do not follow them." John Carroll University's assistant director of admission, Kevin M. Hatgas, *Who Gets In? College Admission Officials Offer Their Advice On College Admissions*, Pittsburg-Post Gazette, 2/15/06.

How To Apply To College See Aresty, pp. 25-97. "Interviewers are under strict orders to be charming and warm, no matter what they think of a candidate. The object of an interview, from the college's point of you, is to give you a terrific experience of their school. It's a recruiting tool." Plus, "...they take up too much time gathering largely useless information..." *On Writing the College Application Essay: The Key to Acceptance and the College of your Choice,* Harry Bauld, Quill (HarperResource), 1987, p. 6; "Often the essay is the only piece of the application that is unique to each student." Case Western Univ's senior assistant in admissions, Diane Feckanin's and Temple's Mary Beth Kurilko's quotes in *Who Gets In? College Admission Officials Offer Their Advice On College Admissions*, Pittsburg-Post Gazette, 2/15/06; "...the level of advocacy for students and the relationship with admissions counselors played a much larger role" this year. *Who Got Into College?* A.M. Chaker, Wall Street Journal, 4/13/06.

Dumb Stuff, SmartMoney.com, *College Planning*, 3/10/06.

SAT & ACT *Another College Drops Standardized Test Requirement for Admissions,* AACRAO Transcript, www.aacrao.org, Heather Zimar, 5/18/05.

Getting The Most Aid, *College Aid Stratagems*, Forbes.com, Ashlea Ebeling, 3/13/06.

Pick A College "...students need to weigh the importance of a four-year finish against other priorities. Second majors, internships, activities and outside study may all enrich the experience but may also add to the time spent getting a degree." "Increasingly, college is shifting from a four-course meal to a collection of credits amassed a la carte." "More students earn credit from more than one college, whether they formally transfer or pick up courses at home over the summer." *Different Paths Lead To A Degree*, Kate Holloway, USA TODAY website, 11/9/05.

Highjacking Scholarships Boston University's website: www.bu.edu/finaid, 5/11/06.

EarlyEarlyEarlyEarlyEarly, *Early Decision: College Experts Forum,* Comments from David Hawsey, www.collegeconfidential.com, 5/11/06.

22 Income Strategies This list is the most relevant. For a list with more narrowly-focused items, see Aresty's book, pp. 101-108; The Princeton Review, Edition 2005, pp. 47-66.

Asset Strategies, *College Aid Stratagems,* Ashlea Ebeling, Forbes.com, 3/13/06; "Retirement funds and pensions are generally not considered assets by both the Federal Methodology and the Institutional Methodology need analysis formulas. You can shelter a considerable portion of your assets by making the maximum contributions to these funds in the years *before* the base year. Likewise, tax-deferred annuities and life insurance policies (e.g., single-premium, universal and whole life insurance policies) are not considered assets by the need analysis system." www.finaid.org/fafsa/maximize, section on Assets, # 7.

529s, UTMAs & UGMAs "They're top-class investments. But they could fail you miserably...funding Coverdells and 529s could be a huge mistake. Confused? Blame it on the bizarre world of college financial aid." *It Pays to Study College-Savings Plans,* Jonathan Clements, Wall Street Journal, 5/10/04; *Paying For College*, Princeton Review, 2005 Edition, p. 32; *The real deal on college savings*, Reuters, posted online, 12/16/05; www.savingforcollege.com; "Ameriprise Financial Inc. has agreed to pay fines after regulators alleged inadequate disclosure to clients, *and other firms have also reached settlements* (Italics added). The Municipal Securities Rulemaking Board, which regulates broker sales of 529 plans, recently agreed to strengthen disclosure and other rules for marketers of the plans." *529 Plans Lose Their Luster*, A.M. Chaker, College Journal website, Wall Street Journal, 3/6/06.

Start A Business During College Years MSN's Jeff Schnepper, moneycentral.msn.com/content/taxes; and www.chrisbirdseminars.com.

Best Kept Secret US News & World Report, 8/29/05, p. 64; *How to cut college costs*, A. M. Chaker, Wall Street Journal, 8/15/2005. Kay M. MCClenney, Director, Community College Survey of Student Engagement, Community College Leadership Program, Univ. of Texas at Austin and her interview on website www.decliningbydegrees.org. Her comments describe the similarities of community colleges with small elite liberal arts colleges; Dr. Gamble's remarks on www.carnegiefoundation.org, posted 5/26/05; the American Association of Community College's website: "Community college students learn in relatively small classes from instructors whose primary responsibility is teaching, not research, and average student-teacher contact time is higher at community colleges than at other higher education institutions." This reads like a description of a small 4-year private college in the 1960s. Are community colleges already "back to the future"? "Amy" posted an insightful statement on her experience with her community college (CC), 5/5/06, on www.insidehighered.com.

After The Award Letter *A helpful family guide to college financing,* Terry Savage, Chicago Sun Times, 5/2/05; alarmingly, the Princeton Review advises, "If you can comfortably afford the amount the school says you must pay, then there is little chance that the school is going to sweeten the deal – it must be pretty good already." This would suggest that schools are already generous. I appeal all awards with one attitude, "It's not enough."

Admissions & US News & World Report, *U. S. News - College Rankings*, 8/29/05, unattributed author at this website, www.collegeconfidential.com. The writer adds, "By all means, though, take advantage of the statistical data they collect!"

College Work-Study Aresty, p. 148.

Wait-Listed *Colleges Accept Wealthier Students off Waiting Lists,* AACRAO Transcript, www.aacrao.org, Heather Zimar, 5/25/05; *On a college wait-list? It helps to be rich,* S. Silverstein, LA Times, 5/21/05.

The 3 Little Pigs Of Financial Aid See tax Form 8863, p. 3. The Katrina Emergency Tax Relief Act of 2005 increased the Hope Credit to a maximum of $3,000, and the Lifetime Credit to $4,000 for those residents in specified counties of Mississippi and Alabama, and in specific parishes of Louisiana.

How Students Flunk IN Quote from interview with Patrick M. Callan, on www.decliningbydegrees.org.

College Money Traps Comments from Peninsula College's newspaper, The Buccaneer, 2/2/05.

6 Survival Tips Originally *The Seven Survival Skills*, from a press release printed in a marketing manual, *How to get a million dollars worth of free publicity*, Paul Hartunian, undated.

Why Pay An Expert? www.nasfaa.org. Click on "Financial Aid Night" and scroll down to "Financial Aid Consultants and Scholarship Search Services Fact Sheet," as of 5/11/06.

Additional Quote Sources

Book Review by George Leef of *Declining by Degrees: Higher Education at Risk*, Hersh and Merrow edit book that examines higher ed's problems. The John William Pope Center for Higher Education Policy website, 1/25/06; *Grade Inflation: It's Not Just an Issue for the Ivy League*, discussion on the Carnegie Foundation website, R. Terry Ervin's post, 4/22/05 4:36:56 pm; *It's time to give teaching more weight*, Jonathan Zimmerman, Christian Science Monitor website, 3/14/06; *The Cambridge Question*, Mortimer B. Zuckerman, US News & World Report, 4/6/06; *Literacy of College Graduates is in Decline,* Lois Romana, Washington Post, 12/25/05; *Ivory Cower: University presidents have lost their dignity,* Victor Davis Hanson, Wall Street Journal, 8/27/05.

Primary Book Sources

How To Pay For College Without Going Broke Reecy Aresty, College Assistance, Inc., 2006. Previously titled, *Getting Into College And Paying For It!* A primary source. Author makes a convincing case for admissions and financial aid as seamless processes. A companion book to this one.

Paying For College Without Going Broke, The Princeton Review, Kalman A. Chany & Geoff Martz, 2005 Edition. Good source for financial aid info, overrated as a primary source.

Paying For College, The Greenes' Guide to Financing Higher Education, Howard R and Matthew W Greene, St Martin's Griffin, 2004. Information on the many legal ways to lower your out-of-pocket costs is markedly absent. Does not meet expectations commensurate with the authors' impressive academic credentials.

How To Go To College Almost For Free, Ben Kaplan, HarperCollins, 2002. The wrong title. It should be, *How You Can Get Into Harvard For Almost Nothing.* If you're applying with similar talents and brains as the author's, this is your guidebook.

Acing the College Application, Michele Hernandez, Ballantine Books, 2002. A good book with this distraction: she tells students not to submit a resume. Two people with equal grades, talents, extracurricular activities - everything - but with few slots open will face this reality: the student with the resume wins.

On Writing the College Application Essay: The Key to Acceptance and the College of your Choice, Harry Bauld, Quill (HarperResource), 1987. Author was an Ivy League admissions director, and this book is witty and instructive.

Secondary Book Sources

Declining by Degrees, Richard H. Hersh and John Merrow, Palgrave Macmillan, 2005.

Shakespeare, Einstein, and the Bottom Line, David L. Kirp, Harvard Univ Press, 2004.

The Professors, David Horowitz, Regnery Publishing, Inc., 2006.

Universities in the Marketplace, Derek Bok, Princeton University Press, 2003.

The Shadow University, Alan Charles Kors & Harvey Silvergate, HarperPerrenial, 1998.

“Rare indeed is the story that questions whether students are learning enough to justify the expense.”

George Leef, Director of the John William Pope Center for Higher Education Policy

ABOUT THE AUTHOR

Paul Lloyd Hemphill is one of the leading advocates in America today for revealing the unknown facts that truly benefit students with college admissions and parents with financial aid.

Since he started his college business, he has helped hundreds of parents in Massachusetts to send their children to the colleges of their choice without spending their life's savings. Paul was once in the same circumstance as his own clients; he wears the financial scars to prove it.

Paul is a highly sought-after, entertaining speaker and media favorite. He provides insider knowledge on how to get the "edge" in the admissions process by *guiding* students, not coaching them to be someone they're not. Parents also enjoy watching Paul help them legally beat the colleges at their own game of skyrocketing costs.

Paul makes his home in Norfolk, MA with one of God's few but better angels, his wife, Ann Marie. He's a graduate of Assumption College (cum laude) with a double-major in philosophy and theology. He's a highly-decorated Vietnam veteran, having been awarded the Bronze Star Medal and the Vietnamese Cross of Gallantry.

Paul's hobby is writing and editing. He writes a monthly newsletter on all matters of college admissions and financial aid, and he edits articles and manuscripts for 2 Civil War historians whose specialty is the battle of Gettysburg.

Before ever knowing of the existence of a FAFSA form, Paul's son John graduated from Salve Regina University, and son Mark is attending the University of Massachusetts at Dartmouth.

After spending over 20 years in marketing, he experienced the college game up close and personal.

Visit his website: www.collegefundingprep.com